HOW TO DRAFT
BASIC PATTERNS

ALSO BY THE AUTHORS

**Designing Apparel through the Flat Pattern,
6th Edition** includes:

- Waists: dart manipulation, stylized darts, flanges, princess line, etc.
- Blouses: tuck-in, overblouses
- Halters & Surplice Waists
- Vests
- Facings
- Buttons & Buttonholes
- Collars: set-in, notched
- Sleeves: set-in, kimono, dolman, raglan
- Skirts: gored, circular, peg-top, wraparound, etc.
- Pants: all length and style variations
- Tab Openings
- Pockets
- Princess Line Garments
- Garments Developed from Dartless Sloper

HOW TO DRAFT BASIC PATTERNS

Fourth Edition

Ernestine Kopp, Professor Emeritus of Apparel Design
Former Chairman: Apparel Design Department
Fashion Institute of Technology

Vittorina Rolfo, Professor Emeritus of Apparel Design
Former Chairman: Apparel Design Department
Fashion Institute of Technology

Beatrice Zelin, Professor Emeritus of Apparel Design
Former Assistant Director of Placement
Fashion Institute of Technology

Lee Gross
Former Instructor: Art Department
Fashion Institute of Technology

FAIRCHILD FASHION & MERCHANDISING GROUP
NEW YORK

How to Draft Basic Patterns provides the principles and instructions for drafting slopers through standard or individual measurements. The slopers developed from this text will generate the most basic structured designs. They are also the foundation to such sub-slopers as the one-dart waist sloper, kimono sloper, raglan sloper, shift sloper, and others all developed in *Designing Apparel through the Flat Pattern,* 6th edition.

The measurements included in this book are measurements used by the Wolf Form Company. However, individual measurements can be substituted provided that they are taken accurately and in the manner illustrated in this text. When using the standard measurements you will find that the completed sloper, when placed on various figures of the same size, will always be properly balanced grainwise. Minor adjustments, however, may be necessary due to the difference in measurements from one manufacturer to another. It is also a fact that the same size dress forms by the same manufacturer vary, depending upon the accuracy of the forms when manufactured.

It should be noted that with ever changing fashions, new silhouettes cause measurements to change and adjustments of the basic sloper become necessary from time to time. The alert patternmaker or designer can readily make these adjustments without sacrificing the balance and fit of the original sloper. For example:

- When padded shoulders are in fashion, the shoulderline of the front and back waist slopers would have to be raised at the end of the shoulder to accommodate the shoulder pads, and the depth of the cap on the basic sleeve would have to be increased to fit the new larger armholes.
- Cinched-in waistlines would require deeper darts and side seam pick-ups.

For more radical changes in the silhouette, it is then advisable to draft a new waist sloper using the new measurements. Although measurements and silhouettes change, the principles of drafting do not.

With the organization of the material in this text, we hope to have fulfilled the need of the many users of the companion text: *Designing Apparel through the Flat Pattern.*

CONTENTS

BASIC INFORMATION NEEDED TO DEVELOP SLOPERS

Sloper is the most popular term used to describe the basic waist, skirt, and sleeve from which *all* designs are developed. They are also called *master patterns, block patterns,* or *foundation patterns.* **Slopers are developed usually without seams,** since seam allowances can sometimes interfere with the proportioning and developing of design variations.

Slopers are also developed with balanced seams so that they may be used for matching of stripes, checks and plaids.

This unit covers the terminology, identification and proper usage of tools and basic principles applicable to the development of slopers regardless of size, shape or design. The material covered, if carefully applied to any of the projects in this text, will result in the accurate and professional production of slopers. It is advisable to study this unit thoroughly before developing the projects in this text.

Slopers may also be used as patterns. If so, seam and hem allowances must be added.

TERMINOLOGY & PROCEDURES USED TO DEVELOP SLOPERS & PATTERNS

BALANCING

Balancing is the process of matching two seams to establish grainline, seam length, and amount of flare or fullness introduced.

CLOSE & CUP

Close and cup is a term used when trueing darts. One dartline is creased. The creased fold is matched to the opposite dartline and dart is pinned closed. Pattern is folded under at apex or dart point, and seamline crossing dart is trued.

COPY

A thin patternmaking paper is placed over the draft or sections of the draft, and pinned to prevent shifting. Using proper tools, lines, crossmarks, etc., are copied.

CROSSMARK

A short line which crosses a seamline, dartline, tuck line, etc. Used to indicate seam joining, matching points or stitching points.

CUT

Cut on inside of pencil line. This refers only to cutting finished outside lines on slopers and patterns to retain the original fit when copying and outlining.

DART UNDERLAY

A dart is a "V" shaped stitched fold starting at a certain width at one end and tapering to a point at the other end. The area between the stitched lines is called *underlay* or *pick up*.

DOT

A small round mark used to denote a specific point on a sloper or pattern, often indicated with an awl.

NOTCHES

Notches are crossmarks transferred from seamline to edge of seam allowance, using a notcher. Notches are used on finished patterns.

OUTLINE

The process of drawing a line along the edge of the sloper or draft without seam allowances.

TRACING

Tracing is the process of transferring pattern lines, using a tracing wheel, onto another sheet (or sheets) of paper or to the opposite side of a folded sheet of paper. Folded draft is opened or sheets are separated and traced lines are pencilled in with the proper tools.

TRUEING

The process of connecting all points on a pattern and checking for accuracy of measurements, dartlines, seamlines, crossmarks, shape of seamlines, etc.

TOOLS & MATERIALS NEEDED TO DEVELOP SLOPERS & PATTERNS

The following list defines the tools and materials needed to develop slopers and patterns discussed in this text. The uses refer specifically to the development of slopers and patterns.

AWL

A pointed tool with a wooden handle. Used to pierce small holes such as to indicate apex and points of darts.

COMPASS

A tool consisting of two rods, one sharply pointed and the other equipped with a drawing end; joined at the top with a hinge to provide an adjustable movement. Compasses are available in various sizes to draw circles of different measurements. Used to make curved or circular lines such as for circular skirts and ruffles.

DESIGNER'S NECKLINE CURVE

A clear plastic measuring tool of two curves delineating front and back necklines. Each curve is marked in specific segments corresponding to garment sizes. Used to draft accurately the shape and fit of a neckline. Refer to page 6 for complete instructions on how to use curve.

FRENCH CURVE

A plastic tool shaped into a curve at one end. Used to mark armholes and necklines.

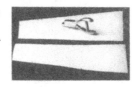

HIP CURVE RULER

A wooden or metal 24-inch (61.95-cm) ruler that is shaped into a curve at one end. Used to curve hiplines on skirts and slacks.

L-SQUARE

A wooden, metal or plastic ruler with one side longer than the other. Sides form an "L" as the name implies. Used: (1) to draft slopers and patterns; (2) to establish length and grainlines on slopers and patterns.

MUSLIN

A plain weave fabric made from bleached or unbleached carded yarns in a variety of weights. The following weights are important to the patternmaker:

1. A coarse weave (not highly sized)—used to test a basic sloper in fabric.

2. A lightweight muslin used to test softly draped garments.

3. A heavyweight, firmly woven muslin—used to test tailored garments such as coats and suits.

NOTCHER

A hand punching tool which produces a 1/16" (0.16 cm) nick in paper or oaktag. Used to establish notches at the outer edge of a seam when pattern is completed.

OAKTAG

A heavyweight paper (Grade 1× or .008), usually beige in color. Used to make basic slopers.

TOOLS & MATERIALS NEEDED TO DEVELOP SLOPERS & PATTERNS

PATTERNMAKING PAPER

A strong, white paper in a variety of widths and weights, available in rolls. Paper must be soft enough to fold at dartlines or seams and able to remain flat when opened. Do not use tissue paper as it will tear easily. A paper with a grid pattern of dots is also available. This type of patternmaking paper is used for markers in the garment industry.

PENCILS

Red, blue and numbers 2 and 3 lead pencils. Used to mark paper or muslin slopers and patterns.

PINS

Size 17 steel satin straight pins. Used to fasten parts and pieces together.

PUSH PINS

A pin approximately ½" (1.27 cm) long with a plastic- or metal-shaped head. Used to secure sloper or pattern pieces to paper.

RULER

A clear plastic, metal or wooden straight edge with clearly marked measurements. It is advisable to have 6", 8", 18" (15.24, 20.32, and 45.72 cm) rulers.

SCISSORS

A cutting instrument at least 9" (22.56 cm) in length. Since paper will dull scissors, it is preferable to have two pairs, one for cutting paper and one for cutting fabric.

TAPEMEASURE

A narrow, firmly woven 60" (152.40 cm) tape with metal tips on each end. Measurements should appear on both sides with 1" (2.54 cm) at alternate ends. This will facilitate working with tape, since it can be picked up at either end.

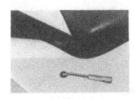

DRESSMAKER'S TRACING PAPER

Paper coated on one side with wax or chalk. It is carbon paper made for the garment industry. Red and blue colors are used for patternmaking to transfer pattern lines onto muslin. White is used to transfer pattern lines onto garment fabric.

TRACING WHEEL

A small hand tool with a serrated or pointed wheel at one end. Used to transfer: (1) one side of the pattern to the other, and (2) pattern lines to muslin or fabric. There are two types of wheels:

1. Dull point—used on fabric (will not damage fabric).

2. Sharp point—used on paper (will not cut paper).

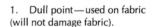

YARDSTICK

A 36" or 45" (91.44 or 114.30 cm) wooden or metal straight edge. Measurements are clearly marked.

HOW TO USE THE
DESIGNER'S NECKLINE CURVE

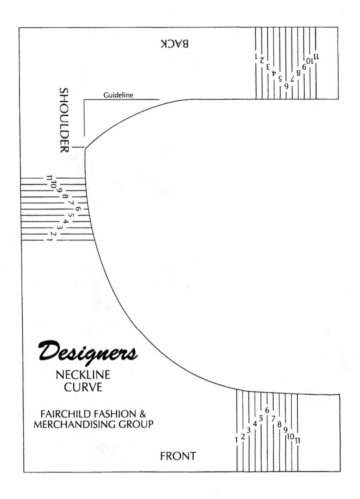

The designer's neckline curve* was developed to promote accuracy in the shape and fit of the neckline.

To measure for depth and width of front neckline, position curve around front of neck shifting curve until identical numbers on the neckline curve touch the shoulder seam and center front of body or model form. For example, size 12 = #7 and #7.

To measure for the width of the back neckline, follow the same procedure until shoulder crossmark touches shoulder seam, and a number sets accurately on center back. For example, size 12 = #7.

When adjusting curve to neckline, *care* should be taken to place center front and center back lines of curve parallel to center front and center back of body or model form.

THE MODEL FORM

FRONT VIEW

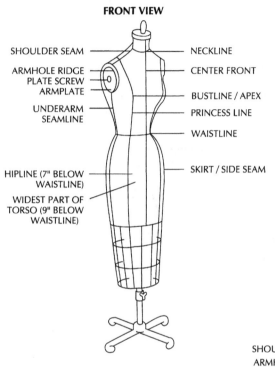

SHOULDER SEAM

ARMHOLE RIDGE
PLATE SCREW
ARMPLATE

UNDERARM
SEAMLINE

NECKLINE

CENTER FRONT

BUSTLINE / APEX

PRINCESS LINE

WAISTLINE

HIPLINE (7" BELOW
WAISTLINE)

WIDEST PART OF
TORSO (9" BELOW
WAISTLINE)

SKIRT / SIDE SEAM

The model form is the duplication of the human torso covered in heavy linen and padded with cotton, set on a movable, height-adjustable stand. It may also be called *figure* or *dress form.*

Seamlines for shoulder, side seam, armhole, center front and center back, waistline, neckline and princess line are indicated on the form.

The industrial form is used in the design room where original designs are draped and developed and in the production room where the patternmaker prepares and tests slopers and patterns for volume production.

BACK VIEW

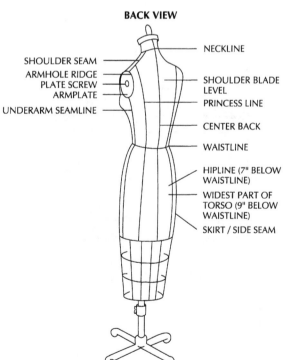

SHOULDER SEAM
ARMHOLE RIDGE
PLATE SCREW
ARMPLATE
UNDERARM SEAMLINE

NECKLINE

SHOULDER BLADE
LEVEL

PRINCESS LINE

CENTER BACK

WAISTLINE

HIPLINE (7" BELOW
WAISTLINE)

WIDEST PART OF
TORSO (9" BELOW
WAISTLINE)

SKIRT / SIDE SEAM

IDENTIFICATION OF SEAMS & DARTS ON BASIC SLOPERS

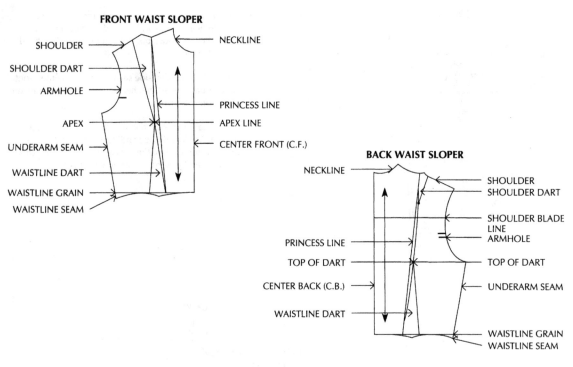

FRONT WAIST SLOPER

SHOULDER
SHOULDER DART
ARMHOLE
APEX
UNDERARM SEAM
WAISTLINE DART
WAISTLINE GRAIN
WAISTLINE SEAM

NECKLINE
PRINCESS LINE
APEX LINE
CENTER FRONT (C.F.)

BACK WAIST SLOPER

NECKLINE
PRINCESS LINE
TOP OF DART
CENTER BACK (C.B.)
WAISTLINE DART

SHOULDER
SHOULDER DART
SHOULDER BLADE LINE
ARMHOLE
TOP OF DART
UNDERARM SEAM
WAISTLINE GRAIN
WAISTLINE SEAM

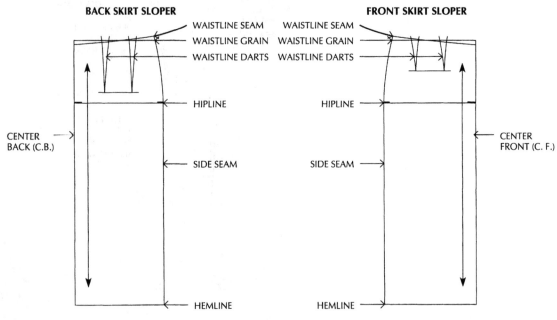

BACK SKIRT SLOPER

WAISTLINE SEAM
WAISTLINE GRAIN
WAISTLINE DARTS
HIPLINE
CENTER BACK (C.B.)
SIDE SEAM
HEMLINE

FRONT SKIRT SLOPER

WAISTLINE SEAM
WAISTLINE GRAIN
WAISTLINE DARTS
HIPLINE
CENTER FRONT (C. F.)
SIDE SEAM
HEMLINE

IDENTIFICATION OF SEAMS & DARTS ON BASIC SLOPERS

FITTED SLEEVE SLOPER

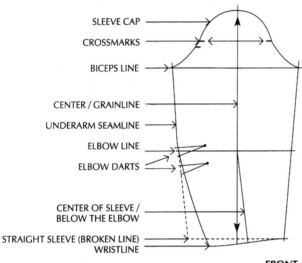

SLEEVE CAP

CROSSMARKS

BICEPS LINE

CENTER / GRAINLINE

UNDERARM SEAMLINE

ELBOW LINE

ELBOW DARTS

CENTER OF SLEEVE /
BELOW THE ELBOW

STRAIGHT SLEEVE (BROKEN LINE)
WRISTLINE

FRONT AND BACK SLACKS SLOPER

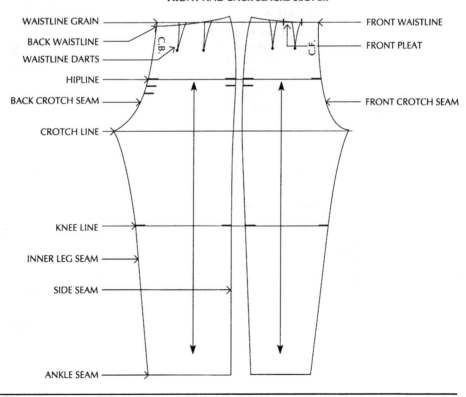

WAISTLINE GRAIN

BACK WAISTLINE

WAISTLINE DARTS

HIPLINE

BACK CROTCH SEAM

CROTCH LINE

KNEE LINE

INNER LEG SEAM

SIDE SEAM

ANKLE SEAM

C.B.

C.F.

FRONT WAISTLINE

FRONT PLEAT

FRONT CROTCH SEAM

PREPARATION OF MUSLIN FOR TESTING SLOPERS & PATTERNS

When testing slopers in muslin, it is important to block and press properly the muslin used, so that lengthwise (selvage) and crosswise grains are at right angles to each other.

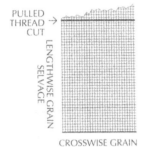

FIGURE 1

If upper edge of muslin is not cut on grain, adjust by tearing or pulling one of the woven threads. Cut on the pulled thread line.

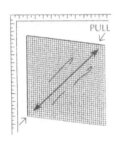

FIGURE 2

On this piece of muslin grains are true on all sides. Muslin must be blocked so that lengthwise and crosswise grains are at *perfect* right angles to each other. Pull muslin in the direction illustrated by arrows.

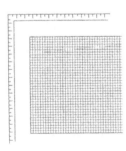

FIGURE 3

Muslin is blocked and pressed, and ready for cutting.

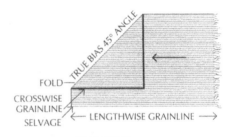

FIGURE 4

Muslin illustrated has tightly woven selvage. Use any of the following methods to adjust:

1. Cut into selvage every ½" (1.27 cm) to release tension.

2. Cut away selvage and pull muslin upwards.

3. Place sloper or pattern for testing 2" or 3" (5.01 to 7.62 cm) in from selvage.

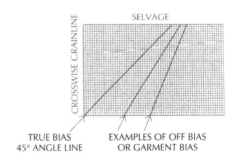

FIGURE 5

To obtain true bias (45° angle) fold muslin matching crosswise to lengthwise grain.

FIGURE 6

Muslin illustrates two lines not on true bias. They are referred to as *off bias* or *garment bias.*

MEASUREMENTS FOR DRAFTING SLOPERS

This text is based entirely on industrial methods where slopers are developed from standard model forms. All major seamlines are indicated on forms to facilitate taking measurements (see HOW TO ANALYZE & CORRECT DRESS FORM SEAMLINES BEFORE TAKING MEASUREMENTS).

However, if body measurements are desired for a specific shape or individual, the procedure for taking measurements becomes more involved. It is more difficult to take measurements on the body than on a dress form, because the lines on the body are not as clearly defined as they are on the dress form. The body also has a built-in elasticity and measurements change as the person inhales and exhales. Also body measurements must be taken by another individual who should exercise utmost care and accuracy in establishing the measuring lines and points similar to those found on the dress form.

Body measurements must be taken over the proper foundation garments such as a bra or one-piece fitted foundation garment. Leotards worn over foundation garments will facilitate the taking of measurements.

Note: It is advisable to check body measurements with the MEASUREMENT CHARTS included in this text. If the measurements appear approximately the same, use the standard measurements and make the slight adjustment when fitting the muslin.

STANDARD MEASUREMENT CHART FOR SLEEVES

Note: 1. All necessary ease has been included in the following measurements. *2.* Measurements subject to change due to changes in styling trends, etc.

SIZES	5	7	9	11	13	15
CAP HEIGHT inches (cm)	5¾ (14.61)	5⅞ (14.92)	6 (15.24)	6⅛ (15.56)	6¼ (15.88)	6⅜ (16.19)
BICEPS CIRCUMFERENCE inches	11¼	11¾	12¼	12¾	13¼	13¾
UNDERARM LENGTH inches	16	16¼	16½	16¾	17	17¼
ELBOW CIRCUMFERENCE inches (cm)	9½ (24.13)	10 (25.40)	10½ (26.67)	11 (27.94)	11½ (29.21)	12 (30.48)
ELBOW DART inches (cm)	1⅛ (2.86)	1¼ (3.18)	1⅜ (3.49)	1½ (3.81)	1⅝ (4.13)	1¾ (4.45)
WRIST CIRCUMFERENCE inches (cm)	6¼ (15.88)	6½ (16.51)	6¾ (17.15)	7 (17.78)	7¼ (18.42)	7½ (19.05)

Note: 1. All necessary ease has been included in the following measurements. *2.* Measurements subject to change due to changes in styling trends, etc.

SIZES	6	8	10	12	14	16	18
CAP HEIGHT inches (cm)	5⅞ (14.92)	6 (15.24)	6⅛ (15.56)	6¼ (15.88)	6⅜ (16.19)	6½ (16.51)	6⅝ (16.83)
BICEPS CIRCUMFERENCE inches (cm)	11½ (29.21)	12 (30.48)	12½ (31.75)	13 (33.02)	13½ (34.29)	14 (35.56)	14½ (36.83)
UNDERARM LENGTH inches (cm)	16¼ (41.28)	16½ (41.91)	16¾ (42.55)	17 (43.18)	17¼ (43.82)	17½ (44.45)	17¾ (45.09)
ELBOW CIRCUMFERENCE inches (cm)	9¾ (24.77)	10¼ (26.04)	10¾ (27.31)	11¼ (28.58)	11¾ (29.85)	12¼ (31.12)	12¾ (32.39)
ELBOW DART inches (cm)	1⅛ (2.86)	1¼ (3.18)	1⅜ (3.49)	1½ (3.81)	1⅝ (4.13)	1¾ (4.45)	1⅞ (4.76)
WRIST CIRCUMFERENCE inches (cm)	6⅜ (16.19)	6⅝ (16.83)	6⅞ (17.46)	7⅛ (18.10)	7⅜ (18.73)	7⅝ (19.37)	7⅞ (20.00)

SAMPLE WORKSHEET FOR SLEEVE MEASUREMENTS

	ARM MEASUREMENT	EASE* (PLUS OR MINUS)	FINAL MEASUREMENTS
CAP HEIGHT		+1½" (3.81 cm)	
UNDERARM LENGTH		-1" (2.54 cm)	
BICEPS CIRCUMFERENCE		+2" (5.08 cm)	
ELBOW CIRCUMFERENCE		+1" (2.54 cm)	
WRIST CIRCUMFERENCE		+¼" (0.64 cm)	
ELBOW DART	REFER TO STANDARD MEASUREMENT CHART FOR SLEEVES		

Note: If the STANDARD MEASUREMENT CHART FOR SLEEVES is used, it is not necessary to "plus or minus" since it has been included.

STANDARD DRESS FORM MEASUREMENT CHART FOR WAISTS & SKIRTS*

Note: 1. All necessary ease has been included in the following measurements. *2.* Measurements subject to change due to changes in styling trends, etc.

	SIZES	6	8	10	12	14	16	18
FRONT WAIST	FRONT LENGTH (from shoulder/neck intersection to waist) inches (cm)	16 3/8 (41.59)	16 5/8 (42.23)	16 7/8 (42.86)	17 1/8 (43.50)	17 3/8 (44.13)	17 5/8 (44.77)	17 7/8 (45.50)
FRONT WAIST	WIDTH OF BUST (1" (2.54 cm) below armplate) inches (cm)	9 5/8 (24.45)	9 7/8 (25.08)	10 1/8 (25.72)	10 1/2 (26.67)	10 7/8 (27.62)	11 1/4 (28.58)	11 5/8 (29.53)
FRONT WAIST	NECKLINE CURVE PLACEMENT Center Front Number / Shoulder Number	4 / 4	5 / 5	6 / 6	7 / 7	8 / 8	9 / 9	10 / 10
FRONT WAIST	APEX inches (cm)	3 3/4 (9.53)	3 7/8 (9.84)	4 (10.16)	4 1/8 (10.48)	4 1/4 (10.80)	4 3/8 (11.11)	4 1/2 (11.43)
FRONT WAIST	UNDERARM SEAM (1" (2.54 cm) below armplate) inches (cm)	7 1/4 (18.42)	7 3/8 (18.73)	7 1/2 (19.05)	7 5/8 (19.37)	7 3/4 (19.69)	7 7/8 (20.00)	8 (20.32)
FRONT WAIST	FRONT WAISTLINE inches (cm)	6 1/4 (15.88)	6 1/2 (16.51)	6 3/4 (17.15)	7 1/8 (18.10)	7 3/8 (18.73)	7 7/8 (20.00)	8 1/4 (20.96)
FRONT WAIST	WAISTLINE TO SHOULDER inches (cm)	13 1/2 (34.29)	13 3/4 (34.93)	14 (35.56)	14 1/4 (36.20)	14 1/2 (36.83)	14 5/8 (37.15)	14 3/4 (37.47)
FRONT WAIST	SHOULDER LENGTH inches (cm)	4 5/8 (11.75)	4 3/4 (12.07)	4 7/8 (12.38)	5 (12.70)	5 1/8 (13.02)	5 1/4 (13.34)	5 3/8 (13.65)
BACK WAIST	WIDTH OF BACK (1" (2.54 cm) below armplate) inches (cm)	8 5/8 (21.91)	8 7/8 (22.54)	9 1/8 (23.18)	9 1/2 (24.13)	9 7/8 (25.08)	10 1/4 (26.04)	10 5/8 (26.99)
BACK WAIST	CENTER BACK LENGTH inches (cm)	15 3/4 (40.01)	16 (40.64)	16 1/4 (41.28)	16 1/2 (41.91)	16 3/4 (42.55)	17 (43.18)	17 1/4 (43.82)
BACK WAIST	BACK WAISTLINE inches (cm)	5 3/4 (14.61)	6 (15.24)	6 1/4 (15.88)	6 5/8 (16.83)	7 (17.78)	7 3/8 (18.73)	7 3/4 (19.69)
BACK WAIST	SHOULDER BLADE inches (cm)	7 (17.78)	7 1/8 (18.10)	7 1/4 (18.42)	7 7/16 (18.89)	7 5/8 (19.37)	7 13/16 (19.84)	8 (20.32)
BACK WAIST	NECKLINE CURVE PLACEMENT Center Back Number	4	5	6	7	8	9	10
SKIRT	CENTER FRONT LENGTH	USE PREVAILING OR DESIRED LENGTH						
SKIRT	FRONT HIPLINE (9" (22.86 cm) below waistline) inches (cm)	8 5/8 (21.91)	8 7/8 (22.54)	9 1/8 (23.18)	9 1/2 (24.13)	9 7/8 (25.08)	10 1/4 (26.04)	10 5/8 (26.99)
SKIRT	BACK HIPLINE (9" (22.86 cm) below waistline) inches (cm)	8 7/8 (22.54)	9 1/8 (23.18)	9 3/8 (23.81)	9 3/4 (24.77)	10 1/8 (25.72)	10 1/2 (26.67)	10 7/8 (27.62)

* All measurements used in this chart are based on measurements from Wolf Dress Forms.

STANDARD DRESS FORM MEASUREMENT CHART
FOR WAISTS & SKIRTS*

Note: 1. All necessary ease has been included in the following measurements. *2.* Measurements subject to change due to changes in styling trends, etc.

	SIZES	5	7	9	11	13	15
FRONT WAIST	FRONT LENGTH (from shoulder/neck intersection to waist) inches (cm)	16¼ (41.28)	16½ (41.91)	16¾ (42.55)	17 (43.18)	17¼ (43.82)	17½ (44.45)
	WIDTH OF BUST (1" (2.54 cm) below armplate) inches (cm)	9½ (24.13)	9¾ (24.77)	10 (25.40)	10⅜ (26.35)	10¾ (27.31)	11⅛ (28.26)
	NECKLINE CURVE PLACEMENT Center Front Number Shoulder Number	4 4	5 5	6 6	7 7	8 8	9 9
	APEX inches (cm)	3½ (8.89)	3⅝ (9.21)	3¾ (9.53)	3⅞ (9.84)	4 (10.16)	4⅛ (10.48)
	UNDERARM SEAM (1" (2.54 cm) below armplate) inches (cm)	6⅞ (17.46)	7 (17.78)	7⅛ (18.10)	7¼ (18.42)	7⅜ (18.73)	7½ (19.05)
	FRONT WAISTLINE inches (cm)	6⅛ (15.56)	6⅜ (16.19)	6⅝ (16.83)	7 (17.78)	7⅜ (18.73)	7¾ (19.69)
	WAISTLINE TO SHOULDER inches (cm)	13⅛ (33.34)	13⅜ (33.97)	13⅝ (34.61)	13⅞ (35.24)	14 (35.56)	14⅛ (35.88)
	SHOULDER LENGTH inches (cm)	4⅝ (11.75)	4¾ (12.07)	4⅞ (12.38)	5 (12.70)	5⅛ (13.02)	5¼ (13.34)
BACK WAIST	WIDTH OF BACK (1" (2.54 cm) below armplate) inches (cm)	8½ (21.59)	8¾ (22.23)	9 (22.86)	9⅜ (23.81)	9¾ (24.77)	10⅛ (25.72)
	CENTER BACK LENGTH inches (cm)	15½ (39.37)	15¾ (40.01)	16 (40.64)	16¼ (41.28)	16½ (41.91)	16¾ (42.55)
	BACK WAISTLINE inches (cm)	5¾ (14.61)	6 (15.24)	6¼ (15.88)	6⅝ (16.83)	7 (17.78)	7⅜ (18.73)
	SHOULDER BLADE inches (cm)	6⅞ (17.46)	7 (17.78)	7⅛ (18.10)	7⁵⁄₁₆ (18.57)	7½ (19.05)	7¹¹⁄₁₆ (19.53)
	NECKLINE CURVE PLACEMENT Center Back Number	4	5	6	7	8	9
SKIRT	CENTER FRONT LENGTH	USE PREVAILING OR DESIRED LENGTH					
	FRONT HIPLINE (9" (22.86 cm) below waistline) inches (cm)	8⅝ (21.91)	8⅞ (22.54)	9⅛ (23.18)	9½ (24.13)	9⅞ (25.08)	10¼ (26.04)
	BACK HIPLINE (9" (22.86 cm) below waistline) inches (cm)	8⅞ (22.54)	9⅛ (23.18)	9⅜ (23.81)	9¾ (24.77)	10⅛ (25.72)	10½ (26.67)

* All measurements used in this chart are based on measurements from Wolf Dress Forms.

SAMPLE WORKSHEET FOR WAIST & SKIRT DRESS FORM MEASUREMENTS

SIZE_____ MAKE OF DRESS FORM_____ YEAR OF DRESS FORM_____

NAME _____

		FORM MEASUREMENTS	EASE (PLUS OR MINUS)	FINAL MEASUREMENTS
FRONT WAIST	FRONT LENGTH (from shoulder/neckline intersection to waist)			
	WIDTH OF BUST (1" (2.54 cm) below armplate)		+ ½" (1.27 cm)	
	NECKLINE CURVE PLACEMENT (center front and shoulder number)			
	APEX (from center front)			
	UNDERARM SEAM (1" (2.54 cm) below armplate)			
	FRONT WAISTLINE		+ ¼" (0.64 cm)	
	WAISTLINE TO SHOULDER (ridge, not plate)		+ ⅜" (0.95 cm)	
	SHOULDER LENGTH (from ridge to neck)		- ⅛" (0.32 cm)	
BACK WAIST	WIDTH OF BACK (from second dot) Flat Back Semi-rounded Back Rounded Back		+ 1" (2.54 cm) + ¾" (1.91 cm) + ½" (1.27 cm)	
	CENTER BACK LENGTH		+ ⅛" (0.32 cm)	
	BACK WAISTLINE		+ ¼" (0.64 cm)	
	SHOULDER BLADE (to plate)			
	NECKLINE CURVE PLACEMENT (center back number)			
SKIRT	CENTER FRONT LENGTH			
	FRONT HIPLINE (9" (22.96 cm) below waistline — widest part of hip)		+ ⅜" (0.95 cm)	
	BACK HIPLINE (9" (22.96 cm) below waistline — widest part of hip)		+ ⅜" (0.95 cm)	

Note: If the STANDARD DRESS FORM MEASUREMENT CHART is used, it is not necessary to allow for "plus or minus" since it has been included.

16

STANDARD MEASUREMENT CHART FOR SLACKS*

Note: 1. All necessary ease has been included in the following measurements, *except* for crotch depth, which is added and explained in the development of the sloper. *2.* Hip and waist measurements are needed only if slacks are developed without using the skirt or torso slopers. *3,* Measurements subject to change due to changes in styling trends, etc.

SIZES	5	7	9	11	13	15
CROTCH DEPTH						
inches	9¾	10	10¼	10⅝	11	11⅜
(cm)	(24.77)	(25.40)	(26.04)	(26.99)	(27.94)	(28.89)
SIDE SEAM LENGTH						
inches	39½	40	40½	41	41½	42
(cm)	(100.33)	(101.60)	(102.87)	(104.14)	(105.41)	(106.68)
KNEE CIRCUMFERENCE						
inches	13½	14	14½	15	15½	16
(cm)	(34.29)	(35.56)	(36.83)	(38.10)	(39.37)	(40.64)
ANKLE CIRCUMFERENCE						
inches	8½	8¾	9	9¼	9½	9¾
(cm)	(21.59)	(22.23)	(22.86)	(23.50)	(24.13)	(24.77)
FRONT HIPLINE						
inches	8⅝	8⅞	9⅛	9½	9⅞	10¼
(cm)	(21.91)	(22.54)	(23.18)	(24.13)	(25.08)	(26.04)
BACK HIPLINE						
inches	8⅞	9⅛	9⅜	9¾	10⅛	10½
(cm)	(22.54)	(23.18)	(23.81)	(24.77)	(25.72)	(26.67)
FRONT WAISTLINE						
inches	6⅛	6⅜	6⅝	7	7⅜	7¾
(cm)	(15.56)	(16.19)	(16.83)	(17.78)	(18.73)	(19.69)
BACK WAISTLINE						
inches	5¾	6	6¼	6⅝	7	7⅜
(cm)	(14.61)	(15.24)	(15.88)	(16.83)	(17.78)	(18.73)

* All measurements used in this chart are based on measurements from Wolf Dress Forms.

STANDARD MEASUREMENT CHART FOR SLACKS*

Note: 1. All necessary ease has been included in the following measurements, *except* for crotch depth, which is added and explained in the development of the sloper. *2.* Hip and waist measurements are needed only if slacks are developed without using the skirt or torso slopers. *3.* Measurements subject to change due to changes in styling trends, etc.

SIZES	6	8	10	12	14	16	18
CROTCH DEPTH							
inches	10	10¼	10½	10⅞	11¼	11⅝	12
(cm)	(25.40)	(26.04)	(26.67)	(27.62)	(28.58)	(29.53)	(30.48)
SIDE SEAM LENGTH							
inches	39¾	40¼	40¾	41¼	41¾	42¼	42¾
(cm)	(100.97)	(102.24)	(103.51)	(104.78)	(106.05)	(107.32)	(108.59)
KNEE CIRCUMFERENCE							
inches	13½	14	14½	15	15½	16	16½
(cm)	(34.29)	(35.56)	(36.83)	(38.10)	(39.37)	(40.64)	(41.91)
ANKLE CIRCUMFERENCE							
inches	8½	8¾	9	9¼	9½	9¾	10
(cm)	(21.59)	(22.23)	(22.86)	(23.50)	(24.13)	(24.77)	(25.40)
FRONT HIPLINE							
inches	8⅝	8⅞	9⅛	9½	9⅞	10¼	10⅝
(cm)	(21.91)	(22.54)	(23.18)	(24.13)	(25.08)	(26.04)	(26.99)
BACK HIPLINE							
inches	8⅞	9⅛	9⅜	9¾	10⅛	10½	10⅞
(cm)	(22.54)	(23.18)	(23.81)	(24.77)	(25.72)	(26.67)	(27.62)
FRONT WAISTLINE							
inches	6¼	6½	6¾	7⅛	7⅜	7⅞	8¼
(cm)	(15.88)	(16.51)	(17.15)	(18.10)	(18.73)	(20.00)	(20.96)
BACK WAISTLINE							
inches	5¾	6	6¼	6⅝	7	7⅜	7¾
(cm)	(14.61)	(15.24)	(15.88)	(16.83)	(17.78)	(18.73)	(19.69)

* All measurements used in this chart are based on measurements from Wolf Dress Forms.

SAMPLE WORKSHEET FOR SLACK MEASUREMENTS

	SLACK FORM OR INDIVIDUAL MEASUREMENTS	EASE PLUS	FINAL MEASUREMENTS
CROTCH DEPTH			
SIDE SEAM LENGTH			
KNEE CIRCUMFERENCE		+ 1" (2.54 cm)	
ANKLE CIRCUMFERENCE		+ ¼" (0.64 cm)	
FRONT HIPLINE		+ ⅜" (0.95 cm)	
BACK HIPLINE		+ ⅜" (0.95 cm)	
FRONT WAISTLINE		+ ¼" (0.64 cm)	
BACK WAISTLINE		+ ¼" (0.64 cm)	

Note: If the STANDARD MEASUREMENT CHART FOR SLACKS is used, it is not necessary to "plus," since it has been included; *except* for crotch depth, which is added and explained in the development of the sloper.

Note: To achieve a better understanding of where the seamlines and intersections should be placed on the body, refer to sections of taking measurements for drafting waist and skirt slopers in this unit.

NECK & SHOULDER

Place small squares of masking tape at:

1. base of neck at center front;
2. base of neck at center back;
3. base of neck at shoulder intersection;
4. end of shoulder at armhole intersection.

SHOULDER

Apply narrow tape from base of neck to armhole.

WAISTLINE

Place narrow tape around indentation of waistline.

CENTER FRONT & CENTER BACK

Establish a vertical line at center front and at center back with pins or narrow tape.

Note: To accurately divide body take full bust, waist and hip measurements. Divide these measurements in half. Body measurements from center front to center back lines should equal these total measurements.

UNDERARM & SIDE SEAMS

Establish seams with pins or narrow tape down to 9" (22.46 cm) below waistline.

BASE OF NECK

On tape squares, dot the center front, center back, and shoulder points. Use neckline numbers on designer's neckline curve as guides in establishing these points.

To complete taking measurements refer to instructions as given for taking measurements for drafting waist and skirt slopers.

We recommend that all drafted slopers, whether developed from standard model form or body measurements, be tested in muslin. Therefore, prepare an entire garment with a center back opening in muslin. Make adjustments, if needed, on muslin transferring corrections to paper draft.

HOW TO ANALYZE & CORRECT DRESS FORM SEAMLINES BEFORE TAKING MEASUREMENTS

Slight discrepancies are bound to be evident in the production of all types of model forms. Therefore, it is of the utmost importance to analyze the form selected and make any necessary adjustments in order to take accurate measurements for the development of a balanced and well-fitting sloper.

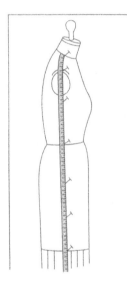

FIGURE 1, SEAMLINE FROM NECK TO END OF TORSO

Pin styling tape or tapemeasure starting from back side of neck and shoulder seam intersection through armplate screw to waistline down to end of torso. If tape does not align with seamline on form adjust seams where necessary by pinning or by drawing a pencil line.

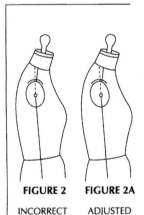

FIGURE 2   FIGURE 2A

INCORRECT   ADJUSTED
PLACEMENT   ARMPLATE
OF ARMHOLE
PLATE

FIGURE 2, ARMPLATE

To take figure measurements properly, armplate should swing slightly towards the front. If armplate does not swing forward as in Figure 2, adjust by loosening plate screw "a fraction" and moving plate slightly towards the front; retighten screw.

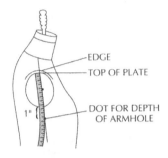

EDGE
TOP OF PLATE
DOT FOR DEPTH OF ARMHOLE
1"

FIGURE 3, ARMHOLE DEPTH

Note: The form manufacturer often uses the same size armplate for as many as three or four form sizes. This causes discrepancies in the depth of the armhole, thus creating problems when setting in a sleeve. To avoid this problem, establish the depth of the armhole for the various sizes by referring to the following measurement chart.

Measure from the top of the armplate the depth of the armhole for size selected. At times, depth of armhole may end at bottom of plate.

Dress Form Sizes	Depth of Armhole
4, 5	4¼" (10.80 cm)
6, 7	4⅜" (11.11 cm)
8, 9	4½" (11.43 cm)
10, 11	4⅝" (11.75 cm)
12, 13	4¾" (12.07 cm)
14, 15	4⅞" (12.38 cm)
16	5" (12.70 cm)
18	5⅛" (13.02 cm)

Note: Measurements listed under *Depth of Armhole* do not include 1" (2.54 cm) armhole ease.

HOW TO ANALYZE & CORRECT DRESS FORM SEAMLINES BEFORE TAKING MEASUREMENTS

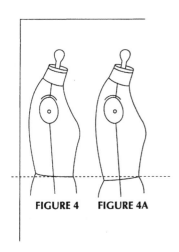

FIGURE 4   **FIGURE 4A**

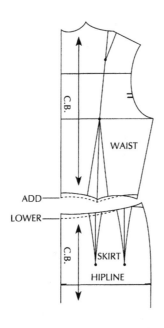

FIGURE 4, WAISTLINE TAPE

The tape defining the waistline on the dress form is usually correct, but occasionally it is not properly placed. In Figure 4, the waistline tape is too high at the center back in relation to the side and front. In this case, adjust tape at center back by dropping tape slightly from side seam to ¼" (0.64 cm) at center back (see *Figure 4A*). This procedure can be applied to a standard form.

Note: If the center back of the form is lower than ¼" (0.64 cm), raise tape. It is important to adjust the tape in order to develop properly the standard sloper as well as to preserve the balance and fit of the sloper.

FIGURE 5

If a longer back is needed, adjustment is made after the basic sloper has been completed and tested. Lower waistline on waist sloper at center back amount desired and lower waistline on skirt sloper the same amount (as illustrated.)

HOW TO TAKE MEASUREMENTS ON BODY & ARM FORM FOR DRAFTING SLEEVE SLOPER

Note: If measuring on arm of dress form, follow the same procedure allowing the same amount of ease.

CAP HEIGHT

Tie tapemeasure or tape around biceps of arm close to armpit. Measure from end of shoulder to top of tape, *plus* 1" (2.54 cm) for lowering of armhole and ½" (1.27 cm) for sleeve cap ease.

SLEEVE LENGTH

Measure from end of shoulder over a bent elbow down to wrist bone.

BICEPS

Measure fullest part of arm *plus* 2" (5.08 cm) for ease.

ELBOW

Measure over elbow bone *plus* 1" (2.54 cm) for ease.

WRIST

Measure over wrist bone *plus* ¼" (0.64 cm) for ease.

HOW TAKE MEASUREMENTS ON DRESS FORM FOR DRAFTING FRONT WAIST SLOPER

Note: 1. Seams, armplate, and waistline on dress form must be checked and corrected if needed before taking measurements. Refer to HOW TO ANALYZE & CORRECT DRESS FORM SEAMLINES BEFORE TAKING MEASUREMENTS. 2. Refer to HOW TO TAKE BODY MEASUREMENTS for body measurements.

FRONT LENGTH
Measure from neckline and shoulder seam intersection down over apex to center of waistline tape.

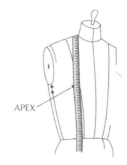

APEX
Measure from apex to center front seam at bustline level. (Princess seam of figure generally falls over center of bust.)

DEPTH OF FRONT NECK/WIDTH OF FRONT NECK
Use designer's neckline curve to find position at center front and shoulder on dress form. Refer to HOW TO USE DESIGNER'S NECKLINE CURVE.

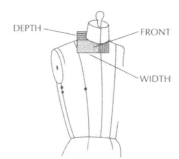

WIDTH OF BUST
Measure from the established armhole dot down 1" (2.54 cm) for armhole ease. Dot. Measure from new underarm seam dot over apex to center front seam of figure *plus* ½" (1.27 cm) for bust and underarm ease.

HOW TO TAKE MEASUREMENTS ON DRESS FORM
FOR DRAFTING FRONT WAIST SLOPER

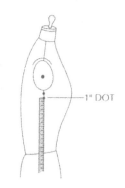

UNDERARM SEAM

Measure from the established armhole dot down to center of waistline tape.

FRONT WAISTLINE

Measure from underarm seam over center of tape to center front seam of figure *plus* ¼" (0.64 cm) for ease.

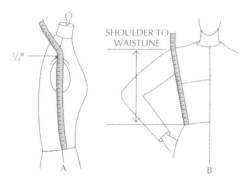

WAISTLINE TO END OF SHOULDER

Figure A: To establish shoulder point, measure ¼" (0.64 cm) in from ridge of armhole and mark with a pencil dot or a pin. Measure from center of waistline tape at underarm seam up over armplate to ¼" (0.64 cm) dot *plus* ⅜" (0.95 cm).

Figure B: To establish shoulder point on body, measure from center of waistline tape at underarm seam around arm up to masking tape at end of shoulder.

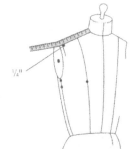

SHOULDER LENGTH

Measure from neckline and shoulder seam intersection to ¼" (0.64 cm) dot *minus* ⅛" (0.32 cm) to compensate for stretch of shoulder after sloper is transferred into muslin. This also allows for blending shoulder seam at armhole intersection.

HOW TO TAKE MEASUREMENTS ON DRESS FORM FOR DRAFTING BACK WAIST SLOPER

BACK WIDTH

Measure from new underarm seam dot (as illustrated) to center back *plus* ease (see figure variations below):

1. 1" (2.54 cm) for flat back.
2. ³/₄" (1.91 cm) for semi-rounded back.
3. ¹/₂" (1.27 cm) for full-rounded back.

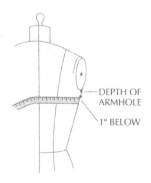

— DEPTH OF ARMHOLE

1" BELOW

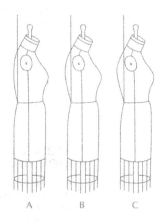

A   B   C

BACK LENGTH

Measure from neckline seam down to center of waistline tape *plus* ¹/₈" (0.32 cm) ease. (Ease is for pick-up over shoulder blade.)

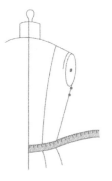

BACK WAISTLINE

Measure from center back seam over center of waistline tape to underarm seam plus ¼" (0.64 cm) for ease.

SHOULDER BLADE

Measure from neckline at center back seam down one-quarter of back length. Dot. At this point measure across back to armplate.

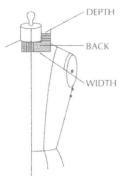

BACK NECK WIDTH

Use designer's neckline curve to find position at center back and shoulder on dress form.

Note: Be sure neckline curve matches established front shoulder and neck points.

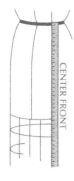

CENTER FRONT LENGTH

Measure from center of waistline tape at center front seam down to desired length.

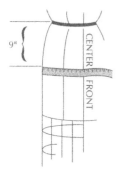

FRONT HIPLINE

Measure from center of waistline tape over side seam down 9" (22.86 cm). Dot. At this point measure across to center front seam *plus* ⅜" (0.95 cm) for ease.

Note: 7" (17.78 cm) is generally considered the hipline and is used in developing slopers, but for proper fit and ease, measurement is taken at 9" (22.86 cm) down which is the broadest part of the hips.

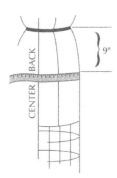

BACK HIPLINE

Measure same as for front hipline.

Note: Width of back and front skirt are usually the same or may vary from ⅛" (0.32 cm) to a scant ¼" (0.64 cm); adjust by compromising. For example: 9⅛"–9¼" (23.18–23.50 cm) change to 9³⁄₁₆" (23.66 cm). If difference is more than ¼" (0.64 cm), do not change.

FRONT & BACK WAISTLINE

Measure same as for waist sloper.

HOW TO TAKE MEASUREMENTS ON BODY FOR DRAFTING SLACK SLOPER

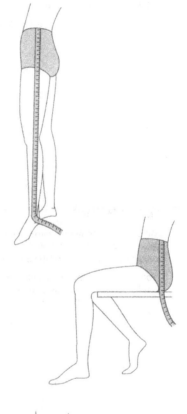

SIDE SEAM LENGTH

Measure from center of waistline tape over hip to ankle.

CROTCH

In seated position, measure from waistline over side of figure to *seat of chair*.

KNEE

Measure over center of knee bone *plus* 1" (2.54 cm) for ease.

ANKLE

Measure just above ankle bone *plus* ¼" (0.64 cm) for ease.

WAISTLINE & HIPLINE

Measure same as for skirt sloper.

HOW TO TAKE MEASUREMENTS ON SLACK FORM
FOR DRAFTING SLACK SLOPER

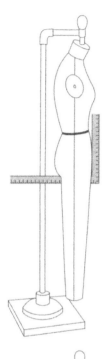

SIDE SEAM LENGTH

Measure same as for slack sloper on body.

KNEE & ANKLE

Measure same as for slack sloper on body.

WAISTLINE & HIPLINE

Measure same as for skirt sloper.

FRONT CROTCH DEPTH

Place L-square between legs of form and note inches on level with waistline.

Note: Since the L-square is 1¼" (3.18 cm) wide, the measurement obtained at waistline level includes 1¼" (3.18 cm) ease.

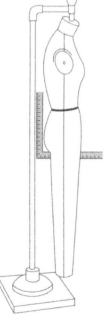

BACK CROTCH DEPTH

Measure same as for front crotch depth.

An accurate set of basic slopers is essential to the development of sub-slopers and patterns. A set of basic slopers includes:

- Fitted Sleeve Sloper
- Straight Sleeve Sloper
- Front and Back Waist Sloper with Shoulder and Waistline Darts
- Front Waist Sloper with Waistline Darts
- Back Waist Sloper with Neckline and Waistline Darts
- Front and Back Skirt Slopers with One Dart
- Front and Back Skirt Slopers with Two Darts
- Front and Back Fitted Torso Sloper with Darts
- Dartless Front and Back Torso Slopers
- Front and Back Slack Sloper
- Jumpsuit Sloper
- Fitted Dress Sloper
- Princess Line Dress Sloper
- Shift Sloper
- Tent Sloper
- Cape Sloper
- Caftan Sloper

Slopers differ from one garment manufacturer to another, and often within the manufacturer. The differences occur because all firms do not use the same measurements for a given size, and firms which do adhere to the same measurements for a given size differ because of the sculpturing of the form within the measurements. However, the principles for developing basic slopers are *not* affected by the differences found in the measurements.

There are two methods used to develop basic slopers:

1. drafting slopers on paper from standard model form or body measurements;
2. transferring a *draped* muslin sloper onto paper (refer to our companion text DESIGNING APPAREL THROUGH THE FLAT PATTERN, 6th edition).

In order to achieve balanced and well-fitting slopers, it is of the utmost importance to be accurate in:

1. taking measurements for worksheets;
2. squaring and trueing lines and crossing intersections;
3. shaping and blending curved lines.

It is also important to have all the required measurements listed on a separate sheet of paper to avoid confusion while drafting slopers. Copy or take measurements in the same sequential order as listed on the measurement charts to simplify the directions for drafting. (Sample measurement worksheets are included in this text.)

Whichever method for drafting slopers is used, all slopers *must* be tested in muslin for accuracy, balanced seamlines, and fit. Corrections made on the muslin must then be transferred to the sloper.

Throughout this text slopers are developed either on the fold of the paper or over accurately drawn rectangle and square lines.

Original slopers which have been completed, tested, and corrected should *never* be altered to develop a specific garment. Original slopers are the *foundation* for developing other slopers and designs. It is recommended that a copy be made of the sloper needed to make the changes necessary for garment or design being developed.

Front View

Back View

DEPTH OF UNDERLAY

ELBOW LINE

BICEPS LINE

TOP OF CAP

FOLD

ONE HALF UNDERARM LENGTH MINUS 1½"

CAP HEIGHT

FIGURE 1

A. Cut paper approximately 16" 28" (40.64 71.12 cm).

B. Fold paper in half lengthwise. Place fold towards you.

C. At top righthand of paper, square a line from fold. Label *top of cap.*

D. From top of capline at fold measure down the depth of cap. Dot. Square a line from dot one-half of biceps measurement and dot. Label *biceps line.*

E. From biceps line at fold measure down one-half of underarm length minus 1½" (3.81 cm). Dot.
Note: Subtract 1½" (3.81 cm) *after* the underarm measurement has been divided in half.

F. Square a line from dot one-half of elbow measurement and dot. Label *elbow line.*

G. From dot at end of elbow line measure down depth of elbow dart underlay. Dot.

FITTED SLEEVE SLOPER

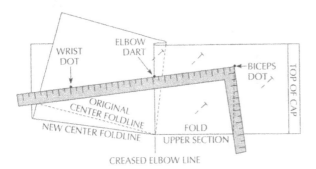

FIGURE 2

A. Open draft and crease elbow line of top layer of paper to fold.

B. Refold upper section of paper and pin to prevent draft from shifting when closing elbow dart.

C. With creased elbow line facing wrist, match creased fold to elbow dart dot. Crease flat and pin through to bottom layer of paper.

Note: Dart underlay at elbow changes the center foldline of sleeve below the elbow. The upper part of sleeve remains the same.

D. With draft in this position, crease new center foldline from elbow down towards wrist. Label *new center foldline.*

E. To locate wrist point, measure from end of biceps line dot through end of elbow dartline dot the underarm sleeve measurement plus ½" (1.27 cm). Dot. See illustration for placement of L-square.

Note: Do not draw this line.

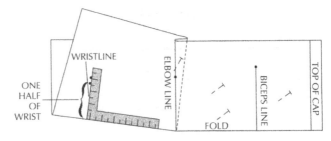

FIGURE 3

From fold of sleeve square a line towards dot one-half of wrist measurement. Dot. Label *wristline.*

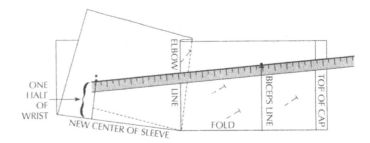

FIGURE 4

Establish underarm seam by connecting adjusted end of wristline dot to biceps. Extend underarm line to top of paper.

Note: Elbow line may become slightly wider or narrower. This will not affect fit of sleeve.

FIGURE 5

A. To develop sleeve cap, crease *upper* section of sleeve in quarters by matching upper section and center fold of sleeve to underarm (broken line).

B. To shape sleeve cap, measure up from biceps line on crease line (broken line) one-half of cap height plus ¾" (1.91 cm). Dot.

C. Measure in from underarm on biceps line 1" (2.54 cm). Dot.

D. With a straight broken line, connect dots.

E. Measure in from center fold on capline ¼" (0.64 cm). Dot.

F. With a straight broken line connect capline and crease line dots.

G. Using French curve, blend armhole (heavier line). See Figure 5A for placement of French curve at cap and underarm.

Note: Armhole curve remains on biceps line for ¼" (0.64 cm) at underarm intersection to retain rounder underarm.

H. With draft folded, trace underarm and a short line on biceps and elbow at underarm seam through to opposite side.

I. With draft folded, cut paper away only at armhole and wristline.

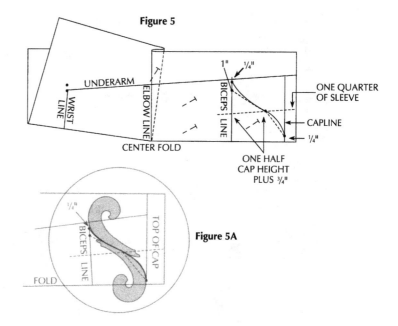

Figure 5

Figure 5A

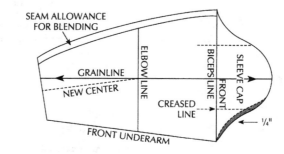

FIGURE 6

A. Open draft. Pencil in traced underarm seam with ruler. Cut on:

    1. front trued underarm seam;

    2. back underarm seam with ½" (1.27 cm) seam allowance (as illustrated).

Note: This seam allowance is needed for trueing seam at elbow see Figure 7).

B. Continue biceps and elbow lines across paper.

C. Label *front* on sleeve cap.

D. To shape front sleeve armhole for proper fit, measure in ¼" (0.64 cm) between creased line and armhole intersection.

E. Blend armhole (broken line) to 1" or 1½" (2.54 or 3.81 cm) above creased line.

FITTED SLEEVE SLOPER

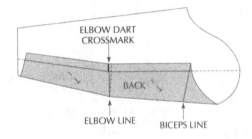

FIGURE 7

A. With blank side of draft facing you, fold upper back of sleeve section matching underarm to center crease line. Crease to elbow line. Pin.

B. Repeat with lower section and crease from wrist to elbow line. Pin.

C. At elbow, fold under dart underlay. Crease, pin, and crossmark for dart depth.

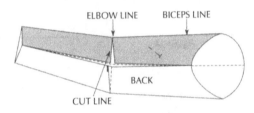

FIGURE 8

A. Fold front sleeve section by matching underarm seam of sleeve and center crease line of sleeve.

B. Cut on elbow line to front fold to facilitate folding the sleeve.

Note: Spread of slash automatically increases back underarm seam. Necessary adjustments will take place in Figure 9.

C. With dart closed, correct the back underarm seam (broken line).

Note: Amount of blending of this line varies depending upon sleeve size.

D. Lift front sleeve section and trim away excess paper on back of sleeve.

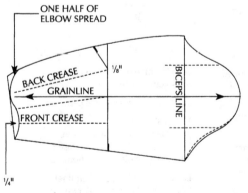

FIGURE 9

A. Open draft. Draw lower dartline to ⅛" (0.32 cm) from creased line.

B. To shape wrist, label *front* and *back crease* (as illustrated).

C. On front crease, measure up ¼" (0.64 cm). Dot.

D. On back underarm seam, measure up one-half the amount of spread at elbow slash (see *Figure 8*). Refold front section of sleeve to obtain correct measurement.

E. Blend wrist curve (heavier line).

F. Draw grainline on original foldline of sleeve.

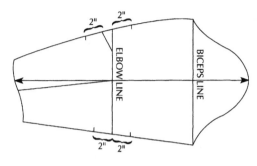

FIGURE 10, SHIRRING ELBOW DART

Note: When using the sleeve sloper as a long, tight-fitting sleeve, it is advisable to convert the elbow dart into two darts or to shirr and shrink the dart fullness out of the sleeve. One dart tends to give the elbow a pointed look. By using two darts or shrinking out the dart, the elbow area takes on a softer and rounder appearance.

A. Place a crossmark 2" (5.08 cm) above and below dartlines (as illustrated).

B. Establish matching crossmarks on front of sleeve measuring down from elbow line and up from elbow line 2" (5.08 cm).

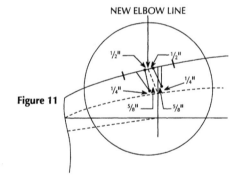

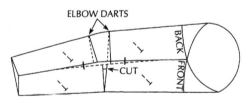

FIGURE 11, CONVERTING ELBOW DART INTO TWO DARTS

A. Establish *new elbow line,* using broken line, indicate inside crease of original dart underlay.

B. Measure at underarm ½" (1.27 cm) above and below *new elbow line.* Mark with dots.

C. Measure on back foldline ⅝" (1.59 cm) above and below *new elbow* line. Mark with dots.

D. Connect dots shortening line ¼" (0.64 cm) in from back fold of sleeve.

E. Form two darts by measuring above and below new dartlines at underarm seam one-half of sloper dart underlay.

F. Refold back sleeve section. Close darts and straighten underarm seam (as in *Figure 8*).

Note: The position of the elbow darts vary depending upon the depth of the original dart underlay—the larger the size of the sleeve the greater the depth of the dart underlay.

FITTED SLEEVE SLOPER

ESTABLISHING CROSSMARKS ON SLEEVE CAP FOR ALL SIZES

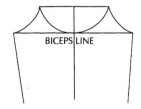

FIGURE 12

A.   Match top of cap to biceps line. Crease.

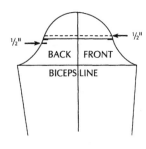

FIGURE 13

A.   Open draft and draw a broken line across crease.

B.   Measure down from broken line towards biceps ½" (1.27 cm). Crossmark.

C.   Draw a line parallel to broken line.

D.   Establish one crossmark on line for front of sleeve. Establish two crossmarks for back of sleeve. One on line and second one ½" (1.27 cm) down (as illustrated).

E.   Draft is now ready for testing in muslin.

F.   Copy draft onto oaktag.

G.   Transfer armhole corrections, if any, to oaktag. If armhole crossmarks need changing, change on *waist* not on sleeve. Cut on all finished lines.

H.   Notch crossmarks and dartlines. With awl indicate end of darts.

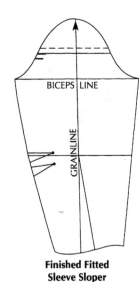

Finished Fitted Sleeve Sloper

Front View

Back View

The straight sleeve sloper simplifies the development of stylized sleeves where the elbow dart is not necessary such as on a bell, shirtwaist, or lantern sleeve. Since the elbow ease has been eliminated, this sloper cannot be used as a long-fitted sleeve *except* when working with knit or stretch fabrics.

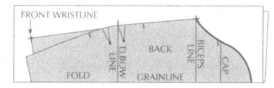

FIGURE 1

A. Use *fitted sleeve sloper.*

B. Cut paper approximately 16" X 28" (40.64 X 71.12 cm).

C. Fold paper in half lengthwise.

D. Fold sloper in half on grainline.

E. With fold of paper towards you and back of sloper face up, place fold of sloper to fold of paper.

F. Outline sleeve cap to underarm seam. Crossmark (heavier line).

G. Holding sloper securely in place, lift back of sloper at armhole. Outline front armhole to underarm seam. Crossmark.

H. Crossmark biceps, elbow, and front wristline (as illustrated).

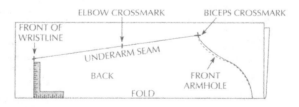

FIGURE 2

A. Remove sloper.

B. On wristline, square a line from fold to front wristline crossmark.

C. Draw a straight line from end of front wristline to biceps crossmark, crossing all intersections. Label *underarm seam.*

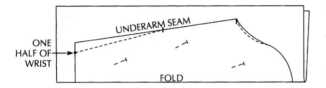

FIGURE 3

A.   At wristline from fold of sleeve, measure one-half of wrist measurement. Dot.

B.   Draw a line from dot to elbow crossmark on underarm seam (broken line).

Note: Both fitted (inner line) and non-fitted (outer line) underarm seamlines are needed from wrist to elbow. The fitted line is used, for example, to develop the lantern sleeve and may also be used for a fitted sleeve on knit or stretch fabrics. The outer line is used for developing the bell, shirtwaist, and other wide bottom sleeves.

C.   Trace front armhole, fitted wristline (broken line) plus short line at elbow, and biceps to opposite side.

D.   Pin draft securely to prevent shifting. Cut wrist, outer underarm seam, and armhole following back armhole line. Open draft and cut away excess paper at front armhole.

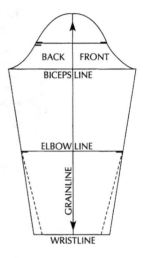

FIGURE 4

A.   Open draft and continue elbow and biceps lines across sleeve. Draw grainline on center fold of sleeve.

B.   Label *front* and *back* (as illustrated).

C.   To establish front and back armhole crossmarks, place fitted sleeve sloper over draft and copy crossmarks.

D.   Draft is now ready for testing in muslin.

E.   Copy draft onto oaktag.

F.   Transfer armhole corrections, if any, to oaktag. If crossmarks need changing, change on *waist* not on sleeve. Cut on all finished lines.

G.   Notch crossmarks and elbow line.

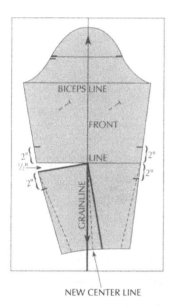

NEW CENTER LINE

FIGURE 5

Note: When using semi-stretch fabrics, some elbow ease may be desired.

A. To obtain elbow ease, copy straight sleeve sloper. True all lines, crossing intersections. Indicate broken lines from wrist to elbow. Cut on all seamlines (as illustrated).

B. Cut sleeve draft on grainline from wristline to elbow line and on elbow line from back underarm seam to grainline (heavier line).

C. Cut another sheet of paper. Draw a line through center. Label *grainline.*

D. Match grainline on sleeve draft to grainline on paper. Pin upper section of sleeve. Overlap sleeve draft at wrist and spread elbow ½" (1.27 cm). Pin.

E. Establish crossmarks for shirring on back underarm 2" (5.08 cm) above elbow line and 2" (5.08 cm) below lower dartline.

F. Establish matching crossmarks in front of sleeve measuring 2" (5.08 cm) above and below elbow line.

G. Outline sleeve, crossmark biceps, elbow and armhole crossmarks.

H. Remove sleeve draft. True all lines and establish new grainline by continuing grainline to wrist (broken line).

Front View

Back View

Note: The use of the straight sleeve sloper is discussed under straight sleeve sloper developed from fitted sleeve sloper.

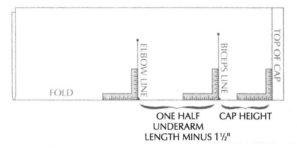

ONE HALF UNDERARM LENGTH MINUS 1½"   CAP HEIGHT

FIGURE 8

A. Cut paper approximately 28" 5 16" (71.12 5 40.64 cm).

B. Fold paper in half lengthwise and place fold towards you.

C. At top righthand of paper, square a line from fold 1" (2.54 cm). Label *top of cap.*

D. From capline at fold of paper measure down the depth of the cap. Dot. Square a line from dot one-half of biceps measurement and dot. Label *biceps line.*

E. From biceps line at fold measure down one-half of underarm length minus 1½" (3.81 cm). Dot.
Note: Subtract 1½" (3.81 cm) *after* the underarm measurement has been divided in half.

F. Square a line from dot one-half of elbow measurement and dot. Label *elbow line.*

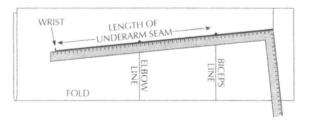

FIGURE 2

To establish wrist point and complete underarm seam, place L-square or yardstick (as illustrated) touching biceps and elbow line dots. Draw line from top of cap to biceps, continuing line length of underarm seam. Dot. Label *wrist.*

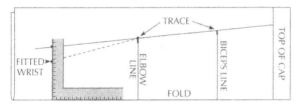

FIGURE 3

A. At wrist square a line from fold of sleeve one-half of wrist measurement. Dot. Continue line to underarm seam.

B. Draw a line from dot to elbow underarm seam intersection (broken line).

Note: Both fitted and nonfitted seamlines are needed from wrist to elbow. The fitted line is used, for example, to develop the lantern sleeve and may also be used for a fitted sleeve on knit or stretch fabrics. The outer line is used for developing the bell, shirtwaist, and other wide bottom sleeves.

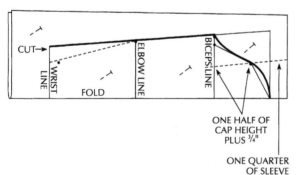

ONE HALF OF CAP HEIGHT PLUS ¾"

ONE QUARTER OF SLEEVE

FIGURE 4

A. To develop sleeve cap refer to Fitted Sleeve Sloper, Figure 5, A through *Note.*

B. Trace fitted wristline plus short lines at elbow and biceps to opposite side.

C. Pin draft securely to prevent shifting when cutting. Cut wrist, outer underarm seam, and armhole.

STRAIGHT SLEEVE SLOPER DEVELOPED FROM MEASUREMENTS

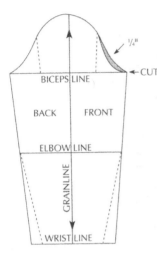

FIGURE 5

A. Open draft and continue elbow and biceps lines across sleeve. Draw grainline on fold of sleeve.

B. Label *front* and *back* (as illustrated).

C. To shape front armhole, measure in ¼" (0.64 cm) between creased line and underarm intersection.

D. Blend armhole (as illustrated) to 1" or 1½" (2.54 or 3.81 cm) above creased line (shaded area). Cut on adjusted line.

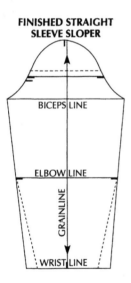

FINISHED STRAIGHT SLEEVE SLOPER

FIGURE 6

A. To establish front and back armhole crossmarks refer to Fitted Sleeve Sloper, Figures 12 and 13.

B. Draft is now ready for testing in muslin.

C. Copy draft onto oaktag.

D. Transfer armhole corrections, if any, to oaktag. If crossmarks need changing, change on *waist* not on sleeve.

E. Notch crossmarks and elbow line.

TWO-DART FRONT & BACK WAIST SLOPER WITH SHOULDER DARTS

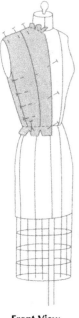

Front View

Back View

DEVELOPING FRONT WAIST

FIGURE 1

A. Cut paper approximately 24" (60.96 cm) square.

B. Fold paper in half, crease sharply and pin. Work with fold of draft away from you.

C. On fold, measure length of waist (allow margins at both ends). Dot.

D. Square a line from each dot width of bust measurements. Dot end of line.

E. Connect these two dots extending lines to edge of paper. Label *center front*.

Note: Recheck length at center front and length of waist at fold—lengths must be the same.

F. Label remaining lines as illustrated.

G. Trace a short line at waistline and center front intersection to opposite side. Repeat at fold.

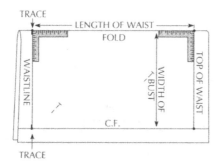

Figure 1

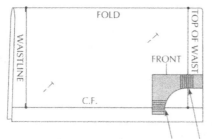

Figure 2

FIGURE 2

A. To develop neckline, place front of designer's neckline curve with determined numbers and guidelines matching at center front and at top of waist (as illustrated). For example: #6 line parallel to top of waist and #6 line parallel to center front.

B. Draw neckline. Label neckline at top of waist, *A* and at center front, *B*.

TWO-DART FRONT & BACK WAIST SLOPER WITH SHOULDER DARTS

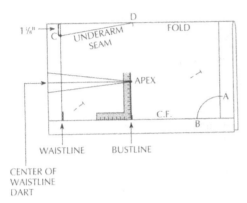

CENTER OF
WAISTLINE
DART

FIGURE 3

A. To establish bustline on center front, divide length from bottom of neckline at B to waistline crossmark. Crossmark.

Note: Position of bustline level may vary depending upon the figure. It may be slightly higher or lower than the halfway mark. Adjustment can be made by raising or lowering bustline desired amount.

B. At crossmark, square a line the apex measurement. Dot. Label *apex.*

C. From apex square a line down and through waistline to edge of paper (line must be parallel to center front). Label *center of waistline dart.*

D. At waistline from fold measure in 1⅜" (3.49 cm). Dot. Label *C.*

E. Draw underarm seam from C to point on fold of paper to equal underarm length (as illustrated). Label *D.*

F. To determine depth of dart underlay, take the *front waistline worksheet measurement* and subtract from *draft measurement.* Draft measurement equals distance between center front and *C.*

Example

8½" (21.59 cm)	=	draft waistline measurement
-6¼" (15.88 cm)	=	worksheet measurement
2¼" (5.72 cm)	=	dart underlay

G. On waistline divide depth of dart underlay evenly on each side of dartline. Draw lines extending through waistline and up to apex.

FIGURE 4

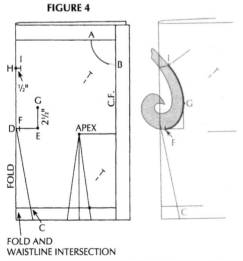

FOLD AND
WAISTLINE INTERSECTION

FIGURE 4

A. To develop armhole, square a line at D from fold length indicated below by size of form used. Dot and label *E.*

SIZES	LENGTH
4, 5	2" (5.08 cm)
6, 7	2¹/₁₆" (5.24 cm)
8, 9	2⅛" (5.40 cm)
10, 11	2³/₁₆" (5.56 cm)
12, 13	2¼" (5.72 cm)
14, 15	2⁵/₁₆" (5.88 cm)
16	2⅜" (6.03 cm)
18	2⁷/₁₆" (6.19 cm)

B. On squared line from D, measure ¼" (0.64 cm). Crossmark. Label *F.*

C. Square a line from E up 2½" (6.35 cm). Dot. Label *G.*

D. At fold and waistline intersection, measure up the measurement obtained from waistline to end of shoulder. Dot. Label *H.*

E. Square a line at H from fold ½" (1.27 cm). Label *I.*

F. Place French curve touching *F, G,* and *I.* Draw in armhole (heavier line in Figure 4A).

50

TWO-DART FRONT & BACK WAIST SLOPER WITH SHOULDER DARTS

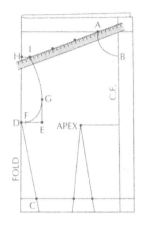

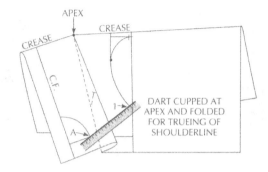

FIGURE 5

A. To develop shoulderline and shoulder dart, place ruler at I and A. Do not draw line.

B. From I measure one-half of shoulder *minus* ¹⁄₁₆" (0.16 cm) and dot.

C. From A measure one-half of shoulder *plus* ¹⁄₁₆" (0.16 cm) and dot. Remove ruler.

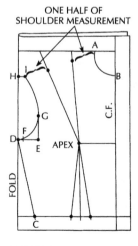

FIGURE 6

Connect dots to apex, drawing lines through dots.

FIGURE 7

A. Open draft and crease line nearest to neckline. Close dart by cupping paper at apex. Match creased fold to dartline nearest armhole. Crease flat and pin.

B. With dart closed, recheck if shoulder dart is centered. Adjust if necessary. Connect dots for shoulderline (heavier line).

C. With a tracing wheel, trace shoulderline through dart underlay.

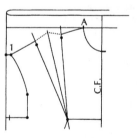

FIGURE 8

Open draft and draw in traced line.

TWO-DART FRONT & BACK WAIST SLOPER WITH SHOULDER DARTS

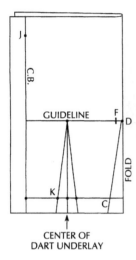

CENTER OF
DART UNDERLAY

DEVELOPING BACK WAIST

FIGURE 9

A.   Refold draft to original position. Trace through waistline and underarm seam C to D and across to F.

B.   Turn draft over to opposite side. Pencil in all traced lines and connect traced back waistline to fold.

C.   From *fold* at waistline and at top of draft, measure across width of back. Dot. Draw a line connecting dots, extending line to edge of paper. Recheck line—it must be parallel to fold. Label *center back*.

D.   On center back line measure up from waistline length of back and dot. Label *J*.

E.   At D square a line from fold to center back. Label *guideline* for top of dart.

F.   To establish waistline dart, measure from center back and waistline intersection same amount as from center front to first dartline. Dot. Label *K*.

G.   To obtain depth of dart underlay follow same procedure as for front waistline dart.

H.   Measure from K towards underarm seam depth of dart underlay. Dot.

I.   Dot center of dart underlay and square a line from dot up to guideline. Draw dartlines from waistline dots to guideline (as illustrated).

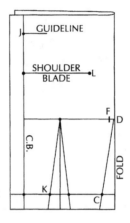

FIGURE 10

A.   From J measure down one-quarter of center back length and dot.

B.   Square a line from dot measurement for shoulder blade. Dot. Label *L*.

C.   From J square a *guide line* approximately 3" (7.62 cm) across draft.

GUIDELINE

FIGURE 11

A.   At intersection of center back and J, place back of designer's neckline curve with determined number and guideline matching at center back.

B.   Draw neckline. At end of neckline, dot and label *M*.

TWO-DART FRONT & BACK WAIST SLOPER WITH SHOULDER DARTS

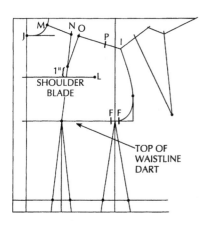

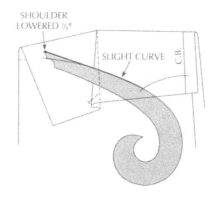

FIGURE 12

A. Open draft. With a straight, lightly drawn guideline connect M to I.

B. From M towards I, measure one-half of shoulder measurement *plus* ⅛" (0.32 cm) for ease. Dot. Label *N*.

C. From N measure ⅝" (1.59 cm) for shoulder dart. Dot. Label *O*.

Note: 1. For rounder back and for sizes 13 and over, make shoulder dart underlay ¾" – 1¼" (1.91 – 3.18 cm) deep. *2.* Final adjustment for depth and length of dart should be made when testing in muslin.

D. From O measure one-half of shoulder *plus* ⅛" (0.32 cm) for ease. Dot. Label *P*.

E. To form shoulder dart, draw a line from N to top of waistline dart.

F. On this line measure up from shoulder blade line 1" (2.54 cm). Dot.

G. Draw a line from dot to O.

FIGURE 13

A. To true dart, crease line nearest center back. Cup at end of dart. Match fold to dartline nearest armhole. Crease flat and pin.

B. Place French curve as illustrated lowering end of shoulder ⅛" (0.32 cm).

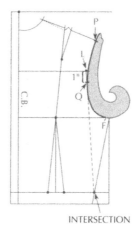

INTERSECTION

C. Draw in shoulder (heavier line).

D. Remove French curve and trace shoulder through dart underlay.

E. Open draft and pencil in traced line.

FIGURE 14

A. To develop back armhole, place ruler at L and at intersection of waistline and underarm seam (broken line).

B. Draw a guideline down from L to waistline (broken line).

C. On guideline from L measure down 1" (2.54 cm). Crossmark. Label *Q*.

D. Place French curve as illustrated and move it into position with curve touching F, Q, and P.

Note: Point at L is automatically blended.

E. Draw in armhole (heavier line).

TWO-DART FRONT & BACK WAIST SLOPER WITH SHOULDER DARTS

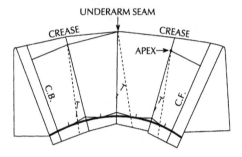

FIGURE 15, TRUEING OF WAISTLINE

A. To facilitate trueing of waistline, draw a line 1" (2.54 cm) below waistline. Cut away excess paper.

B. Crease either side of underarm seam and back and front dartlines nearest to centers and pin as illustrated.

C. Starting with underarm seam, cup draft at underarm and armhole intersection and match creased fold to opposite seamline. Crease flat and pin.

D. Repeat with back and front darts.

E. Blend waistline (heavier line).

Note: Be sure curved line touches original line at points indicated by light crossmarks.

F. With draft in pinned position, accurately trace through dart underlays.

G. Open draft and pencil in traced lines crossing intersections. (Use French curve at underlays.)

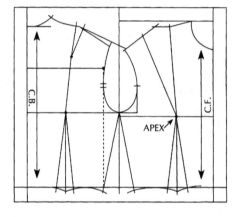

FIGURE 16, ARMHOLE CROSSMARKS

A. To establish armhole crossmarks refer to ESTABLISHING SLEEVE CROSSMARKS ON WAIST ARMHOLES.

B. Establish grainlines parallel to center front and center back.

TWO-DART FRONT & BACK WAIST SLOPER WITH SHOULDER DARTS

FIGURES 17A, 17B, 17C, TRUEING NECKLINE, SHOULDER & ARMHOLE

A. Draft is now ready for testing in muslin. Important points to check and blend are:

1. Neckline and shoulder intersection (Figure 17A).

2. Shoulder and armhole intersection (Figure 17B).

3. Underarm and armhole intersection (Figure 17C).

B. Transfer corrections to draft.

C. Copy draft onto oaktag and cut on all finished lines.

D. Notch all crossmarks and dartlines.

E. With awl indicate apex and end of darts.

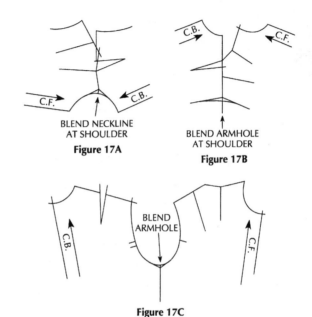

BLEND NECKLINE AT SHOULDER

Figure 17A

BLEND ARMHOLE AT SHOULDER

Figure 17B

BLEND ARMHOLE

Figure 17C

Note: When testing finished sloper in muslin on dress form, waistline ease should be pinned and pinned between underarm seam and dart on both front and back (see dress form sketch).

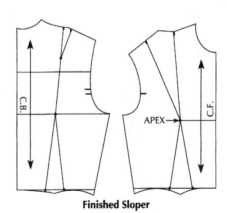

Finished Sloper

ESTABLISHING SLEEVE CROSSMARKS ON WAIST ARMHOLE

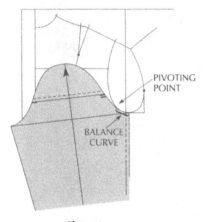

Figure 1

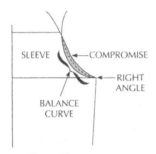

Figure 1A

FIGURES 1 & 1A

To establish sleeve crossmarks on waist armhole, match back of sleeve to back underarm of waist draft extending sleeve sloper ¹⁄₁₆" (0.16 cm) at underarm seam of waist.

Note: Both sleeve and waist armholes should be a balanced curve (Figure 1A). Adjust if necessary. Compromise difference.

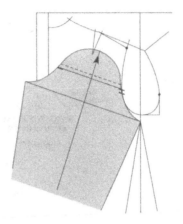

FIGURE 2

A. At pivoting point, hold sleeve at edge of armhole with pin or pencil and pivot sleeve until sleeve crossmarks touch waist armhole. Add crossmarks to waist.

B. Repeat for front of sleeve.

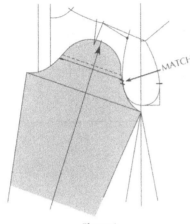

Figure 1

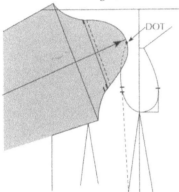

Figure 2

FIGURE 1 & 2

A. To measure sleeve cap for a specific armhole, match back crossmarks of sleeve to back crossmarks of waist armhole.

B. At crossmarks hold sleeve at edge of armhole with pin or pencil and pivot sleeve up towards shoulder intersection. Dot cap of sleeve. Repeat for front.

C. If cap needs adjusting, refer to NOTE above.

D. It is difficult to establish a crossmark on the sleeve cap due to the placement of waist shoulder seam on the form. Therefore, crossmark center of sleeve cap fullness and change crossmark on sleeve, if necessary, to match shoulder seam after testing in muslin.

Note: 1. After testing in muslin, if the other crossmarks need to be changed, change crossmarks on waist *not* on sleeve. 2. If center of sleeve does not match shoulder seam, shoulder seam may be shifted if desired. Refer to ADJUSTING WAIST SHOULDERS TO MATCH CENTER OF SLEEVE. 3. The fullness on the cap of a basic sleeve sloper should be 1" to 1½" (2.54 to 3.81 cm). If it is more, the cap should be reduced. If it is less, the cap should be *increased.*

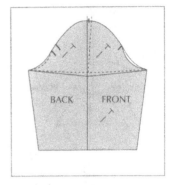

FIGURE 3

A. Start at top of sleeve cap, cut through center of sleeve and across biceps line to, but not through, underarm seams.

B. Overlap top of sleeve cap matching crossmarks.

C. Pin draft onto another sheet of paper. Blend top of sleeve cap, if necessary.

D. Outline sleeve draft completely. Remove draft. True all lines crossing all intersections.

E. Establish grainline on center of sleeve.

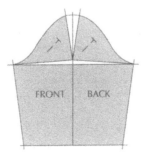

FIGURE 4

To increase cap, follow procedure outlined in Figure 3. The difference would be to spread the sleeve instead of overlapping.

ADJUSTING WAIST SHOULDERS TO MATCH SLEEVE CENTER

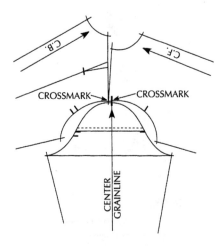

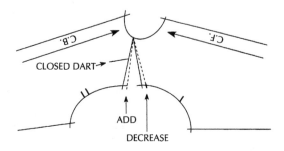

FIGURE 2

On front waist, draw a line from intersection at neck and shoulderline to crossmark at armhole (broken line). Amount eliminated on one side of shoulderline must be added to other side (broken lines).

FIGURE 1

A. When draping or testing muslin for fit of sleeve, center of sleeve (grainline) may not match shoulderline on form. This is due to the placement of the shoulderline on the form.

B. If it is desirable to leave shoulderline as is, crossmark the sleeve to match shoulderline.

C. If desired, shoulder seam may be changed to match center of sleeve. This is often done to facilitate production.

D. To change shoulderline, crossmark the waist to match center of sleeve.

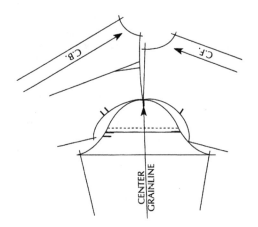

FIGURE 3

This diagram illustrates center of sleeve crossmark matching adjusted shoulderline.

ADJUSTING WAIST SHOULDERS & SLEEVE CAP FOR INTRODUCTION OF SHOULDER PADS

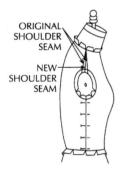

ORIGINAL SHOULDER SEAM

NEW SHOULDER SEAM

FIGURE 1

A. Copy waist sloper in muslin allowing 1½" (3.81 cm) seam allowance on shoulder.

B. Position shoulder pad on form and pin securely.

C. Place muslin waist sloper on form with shoulder seam open to nothing at neck and shoulder intersection.

D. Adjust shoulder over pad and pin.

Note: Amount of spread depends upon thickness of pad.

Blend armhole line on adjusted shoulder.

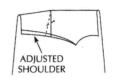

ADJUSTED SHOULDER

Finished Waist & Sleeve Slopers

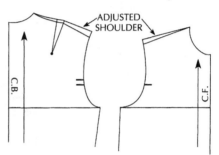

ADJUSTED SHOULDER

C.B.

C.F.

ADJUSTED SLEEVE CAP

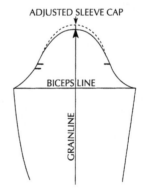

BICEPS LINE

GRAINLINE

FIGURE 2

A. Copy sleeve in muslin allowing 1½" (3.81 cm) seam allowance at top of cap. Notch seam at crossmarks.

B. Pin under part of sleeve to waist armhole up to back and front crossmarks.

C. Balance upper part of cap and pin at center of shoulder spread without turning under seam allowance (Figure 2).

D. Indicate new cap line on sleeve (broken line).

Note: If shoulder pad is extremely thick, the sleeve cap may have to be increased in width as well as in length.

FIGURE 3

A. Remove waist sloper from form and draw in new shoulderline.

B. If original slopers include shoulder darts, trace shoulderline through dart underlay.

C. Copy a new set of slopers and transfer corrections to the new set. *Do not* destroy original slopers.

ADJUSTING WAIST SLOPER TO DEVELOP CERTAIN GARMENTS

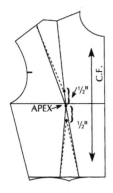

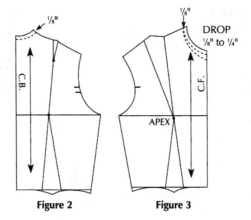

Figure 2   **Figure 3**

FIGURE 1

Note: When the two-dart front waist sloper is used as a dress pattern, the shoulder dart may be shortened across the bustline for ease. If more ease is desired, waistline dart may also be shortened.

A. To shorten shoulder dart, measure up from apex on dartline nearest neckline ½" (1.27 cm). Dot. Draw a line from dot to dartline nearest armhole for new dartline (broken line).

B. To shorten waistline dart, measure down from top and at center of dart ½" (1.27 cm). Dot. Draw two dartlines from dot to waistline for new dart (broken line).

FIGURES 2 & 3

A. When working on slopers used in volume production, the back and front necklines of basic slopers should always be lowered to allow for variations of individual figure types and for bulk of fabric.

B. On back neckline, lower ⅛" (0.32 cm) at center back and at shoulder. Blend new neckline.

C. On front neckline, lower from ⅛" to ¼" (0.32 to 0.64 cm) at center front and ⅛" (0.32 cm) at shoulder. Blend new neckline.

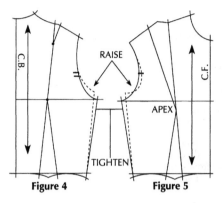

Figure 4   **Figure 5**

FIGURES 4 & 5

A. If a dress sloper is to be used for a sleeveless garment, the following adjustments must be made:

    1. On front and back slopers, tighten underarm seam so that ease will be approximately ¼" (0.64 cm) at armhole. Dot. Draw a line to waistline and underarm intersection (broken line).

    2. Raise armhole so that drop at armhole will be approximately ½" (1.27 cm) below armplate on model form or armpit on body. This is an armhole on a basic sleeveless garment, not on a stylized sleeveless armhole.

B. Blend in back armhole as illustrated (follow broken line).

C. Blend in front armhole. Armhole should be curved inward slightly to release

ONE-DART FRONT WAIST SLOPER

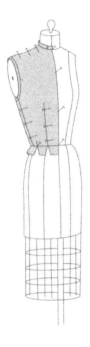

CROSSMARK

D

C

APEX

C.F.

B

A

CROSSMARK

FIGURE 1

A. Use *two-dart front waist sloper.*

B. On sloper label shoulder and waistline dartlines *A, B, C, D* (as illustrated).

C. Cut paper approximately 15" x 25" (38.1 x 63.5 cm).

D. Place sloper on paper. On paper crossmark dartlines A and D. Outline sloper from shoulder at dartline D to neckline, neckline, center front, waistline to dartline A.

E. With awl indicate apex.

D

C

D

C.F.

B

A

A

FIGURE 2

A. Pivoting point is at apex. Hold sloper securely at pivoting point and pivot sloper until dartline C touches crossmark D.

B. On paper crossmark dartline B. Outline sloper from shoulder at dartline D to armhole, armhole, underarm, waistline to dartline B.

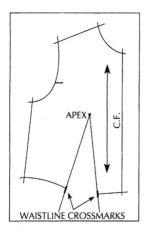

APEX

C.F.

WAISTLINE CROSSMARKS

FIGURE 3

A. Remove sloper. Pencil in apex dot.

B. To form waistline dart, draw a straight line from waistline crossmarks to apex extending dartlines at the waistline.

C. True all lines crossing intersections *except* at waistline dart.

D. Establish grainline parallel to center front.

Finished Sloper

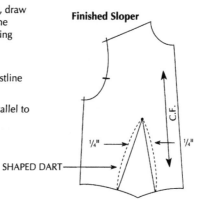

SHAPED DART — ¼" ← → ¼"

C.F.

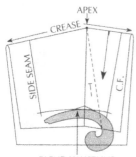

APEX

CREASE

SIDE SEAM

C.F.

BLEND WAISTLINE

FIGURE 4

A. To true waistline dart, crease dartline nearest center front. Close, cup and pin dart (as illustrated). True waistline with French curve. Trace dart underlay on trued waistline to opposite side.

B. With dart closed, cut on seamline.

FIGURE 5

A. Open paper. Pencil in traced dart underlay.

B. For fitted midriff, shape dart as illustrated.

Note: It isn't necessary to test this waist in muslin if two-dart waist sloper was tested and corrections transferred to draft before copying draft onto oaktag sloper.

C. Copy draft onto oaktag and cut on all finished lines.

D. Notch all crossmarks and dartlines.

E. With awl indicate apex or end of dart.

BACK WAIST SLOPER WITH NECKLINE DART

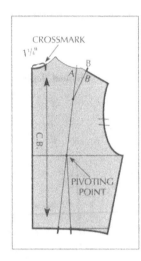

FIGURE 1

A. Use *back waist sloper with shoulder and waistline darts.*

B. To prepare sloper:

    1. Establish position of neckline dart as desired. Crossmark. Illustrated: 1¼" (3.2 cm) from center back.

    2. Label shoulder dartlines *A* and *B* (as illustrated).

C. Cut paper approximately 15" x 25" (38.18 x 63.5 cm).

D. Place sloper on paper. On paper crossmark waist dartlines and neckline crossmark. Outline sloper from shoulder at dartline B to armhole, armhole, underarm, waistline, center back, and neckline to crossmark.

E. With awl indicate top of waistline dart.

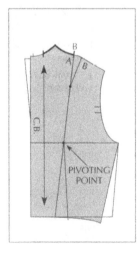

FIGURE 2

A. Pivoting point is at top of waistline dart.

B. Hold sloper at pivoting point and pivot sloper until dartline A meets crossmark B.

C. On paper crossmark at neckline crossmark. Outline sloper from neckline crossmark to shoulder and shoulder to A.

D. Remove sloper. True all lines, crossing all intersections.

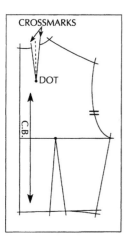

FIGURE 3

A. Establish the center grainline between neckline crossmarks parallel to center back (broken line).

B. Length of neckline dart should equal length of shoulder dart. Establish length of dart on broken line. Dot.

C. To form neckline dart, draw a straight line from neckline crossmarks to dot.

D. True all lines, crossing all intersections.

E. Establish grainline parallel to center back.

Finished Sloper

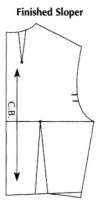

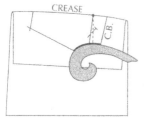

FIGURE 4

To true neckline dart, crease dartline nearest center back. Close, cup, and pin dart. With French curve true neckline. On trued neckline trace dart underlay to opposite side.

FIGURE 5

A. Open paper. Pencil in traced dart underlay.

Note: If back waist sloper with shoulder dart was tested in muslin and corrections transferred to draft before copying draft onto oaktag, it is not necessary to test this waist in muslin.

B. Copy draft onto oaktag and cut on all finished lines.

C. Notch all crossmarks and dartlines.

D. With awl indicate end of darts.

A skirt is defined as (1) the lower part of a dress from the waist to the hem and (2) a separate garment starting at the waist and ending in any length desired.

Skirts play a major role in the classification of a silhouette. If a slim skirt is attached to a bodice, the silhouette achieved is the *sheath*. If the skirt is extended above the waistline and stops below the bustline, it becomes the *empire*. Regardless of the silhouette, skirts are classified as slim, full or shaped. Within these skirt classifications, the degree of width at the hemline and/or waistline varies.

The slim skirt is not necessarily devoid of all fullness. It may have some soft fullness introduced at the waistline and not at the hemline; it may be developed with one or several flat pressed pleats or straight gores. In either case, the skirt retains a slim look.

The full and shaped skirts achieve their width at the waistline or yokeline and/or hemline through the use of gores, pressed or unpressed pleats, gathers, tiers and circles.

Skirt lengths play an important role in the fashion picture. All the lengths illustrated in Skirt Length Variations have been in vogue at one time or another. Most of the skirts in this text have been developed as a mid-calf length, but all the skirts can be interpreted in different lengths. To develop skirts in any of the various lengths illustrated, select suitable style and start with a skirt sloper in the length desired.

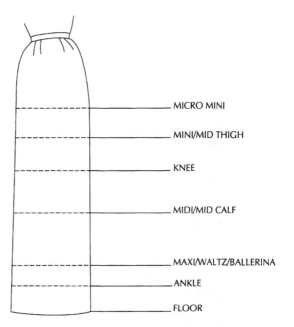

MICRO MINI

MINI/MID THIGH

KNEE

MIDI/MID CALF

MAXI/WALTZ/BALLERINA

ANKLE

FLOOR

SKIRT SLOPER WITH ONE DART

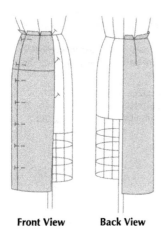

Front View　　**Back View**

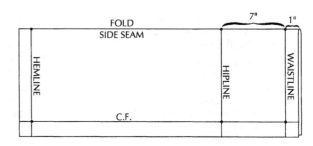

FIGURE 1

A. Cut paper approximately 24" (60.96 cm) wide and length desired plus 3" (7.62 cm).

B. Fold paper in half and crease sharply. Label fold *side seam*.

C. Work with fold of paper away from you.

D. At fold measure down 1" (2.54 cm) and 7" (17.78 cm) and dot. Measure desired length of skirt and dot.

E. At fold square a line from each dot to edge of paper. Label lines as illustrated.

F. From fold at waistline and hemline dots, measure front hip measurement. Dot.

G. Draw a line to connect these dots, extending line to edge of paper. Label *center front*.

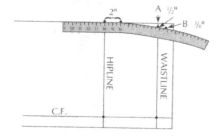

FIGURE 2

A. On waistline at side seam, measure in ½" (1.27 cm). Dot and label *A*.

B. Place a dot on fold 2" (5.08 cm) above hipline.

C. To shape side seam, place hip curve ruler to side seam and hipline touching 2" (5.08 cm) dot and A. Draw in curved hipline from 2" (5.08 cm) dot to waistline extending line ⅜" (0.95 cm) above waistline. Dot and label *B*.

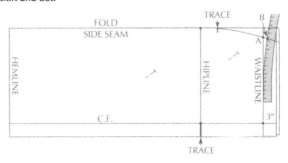

FIGURE 3

A. Shape waistline with hip curve ruler. Draw a slightly curved line from B on waistline.

Note: Curved line must end approximately 3" (7.62 cm) from center front. See illustration for placement of hip curve ruler.

B. Pin paper to prevent shifting and trace through shaped waistline, shaped side seam to

dot. Trace a crossmark at dot on hipline at center front.

C. With paper still pinned, cut through hemline. Lift front section and cut on center front line.

Note: If measurement of back and front skirts are the same, cut on center front line through both layers of paper.

SKIRT SLOPER WITH ONE DART

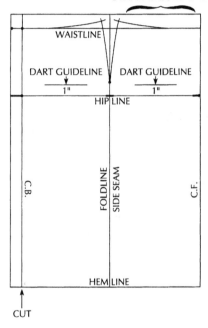

SKIRT WAISTLINE
DRAFT MEASUREMENT

WAISTLINE

DART GUIDELINE ← 1" → DART GUIDELINE ← 1" →

HIP LINE

C.B.

FOLDLINE · SIDE SEAM

C.F.

HEM LINE

↑ CUT

FIGURE 4, SKIRT BACK

A. Open draft and pencil in traced lines (waistline, hipline, shaped side seam dot).

B. Draw a line over side seam foldline.

Note: Steps C and D do not apply if back and front skirt sections are the same in width.

C. Measure from side seam at hemline intersection *back hip* measurement. Dot. Repeat at waistline.

D. Draw a line to connect these dots. Cut and label *center back.*

E. To develop skirt dart, measure up from back and front hipline 1" (2.54 cm). Draw lines parallel to hipline (as illustrated). Label *dart guidelines.*

F. To determine depth of dart underlay:

    1. Measure front waistline on *skirt draft.*

    2. Measure front waistline on *waist sloper* (do not include dart underlay) plus ⅜" (0.95 cm).

Note: 1. This additional ⅜" (0.95 cm) ease allows ¼" (0.64 cm) for skirt waistline ease and ⅛" (0.32 cm) for changes that take place in the final trueing of the waistline. *2.* This ease is also necessary as the skirt usually goes over the waistline of the bodice. If waist goes over skirt, then ease is allowed on waist.

G. Subtract total waistline measurement from skirt draft measurement. The amount leftover is dart underlay.

Example

$$\frac{8⅞"}{(22.54\ cm)} = \text{front waistline measurement on } \textit{skirt draft}$$

$$\frac{- 7⅜"}{(18.83\ cm)} = \text{waistline measurement on } \textit{waist sloper} \text{ plus ⅜" (0.95 cm) ease}$$

$$\frac{1⅛"}{(3.81\ cm)} = \text{dart underlay}$$

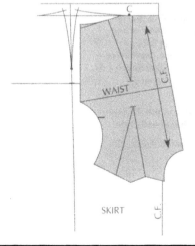

C

WAIST

C.F.

SKIRT · C.F.

FIGURE 5

A. Match waistlines of skirt and waist drafts from center front to first dartline (as illustrated).

B. On skirt draft, place a dot a scant ⅛" (0.32 cm) away from waist dartline measuring towards side seam. Label *C.*

SKIRT SLOPER WITH ONE DART

FIGURE 6

A. Measure from C towards side seam amount of dart underlay and dot. Label *D*.

B. Find center between C and D and square a line down to dart guideline. Recheck that line — it must be parallel to center front.

FIGURE 7

A. Fold on center dartline.

B. Place hip curve ruler (as illustrated) and move it into position until curve touches dart guideline at fold. Draw in dartline (heavier line).

C. Trace dartline through to opposite side. Open draft and pencil in traced line using hip curve ruler as a guide.

D. To develop dart on skirt back, follow same procedure as for front.

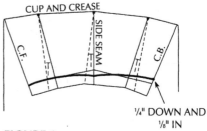

¼" DOWN AND
⅛" IN

FIGURE 8

A. Crease either dartline at side seam and back and front dartlines nearest center.

Note: Crease dart *curved* lines as *straight* lines.

B. Starting with side seam, close dart by cupping draft at crossmark. Match creased line to opposite seamline. Crease flat and pin.

C. Repeat with back and front darts.

D. To true waistline, lower center back ¼" (0.64 cm) and dot. Measure in at back ⅛" (0.32 cm) and dot. Draw a line from center front blending points at dartlines to lowered ¼" (0.64 cm).

E. With draft in this position, trace through dart underlays.

F. Open draft and pencil in traced line.

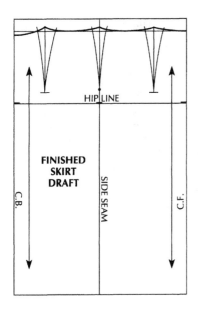

FIGURE 9

A. Establish grainlines parallel to center front and center back.

B. Draft is now ready for testing in muslin.

Note: Skirt may be cut with or without side seams.

C. Transfer waistline or dart corrections if any to draft.

D. Cut paper away at waistline.

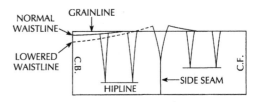

FIGURE 10

A. Copy draft onto oaktag. Cut on all finished lines.

B. Notch hipline and dartlines. With awl indicate end of darts.

Note: 1. If desired, slight additional width may be added at hemline when cutting skirt with a side seam (as illustrated). The additional width at the hemline will prevent seam from puckering when a non-stretch fabric is used. Narrow seams or notching of seams does not solve the problem of puckering. *2.* The additional width may be ½" to 1½" (1.27 to 3.81 cm) for a 28" (71.12 cm) skirt length. For a longer skirt extend the line. The width will widen automatically as the skirt is lengthened and will become narrower as the skirt is shortened.

C. Retain one-piece draft for developing skirts without side seams.

FIGURE 11

Note: When a skirt is made as a separate garment, the waistline must be lowered ½" to 1½" (1.27 to 3.81 cm) as the skirt has a tendency to drop or buckle at the center back waistline.

Lower waistline at center back amount desired and draw a line to nothing at side seam and waistline intersection. See broken line.

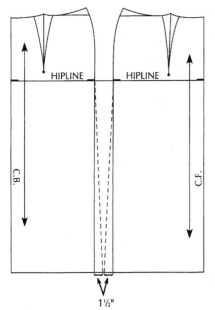

SKIRT SLOPER WITH TWO DARTS

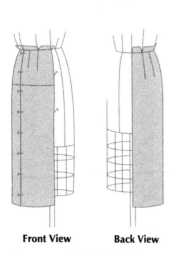

Front View   **Back View**

Two or more darts distribute the fullness across the hipline and tend to give the skirt a smoother fit. The depth of the skirt dart underlays and the length of the darts vary depending upon the shape of the dress form or figure type and the number of darts planned. When more than one dart is planned, the dart underlay is divided into the number of darts desired resulting in smaller and shorter darts.

Regardless of whether one or more darts is used on the skirt, the dart nearest to the center front and center back of the skirt always matches the waistline dart. If two darts are planned, the second dart is usually placed between the side seam and the first dart.

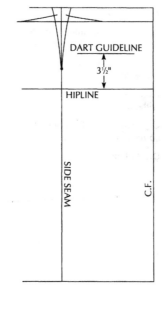

FIGURE 1

A. Copy the one-dart skirt draft (Figure 4). Do not copy darts or to develop draft refer to SKIRT SLOPER WITH ONE DART, FIGURE 1 THROUGH FIGURE 4, D.

B. From front hipline measure up 3½" (8.89 cm) and draw a guideline for end of darts. Label *dart guideline.*

C. To determine depth of dart underlay, refer to SKIRT SLOPER WITH ONE DART, FIGURE 4, F, NOTE, AND G.

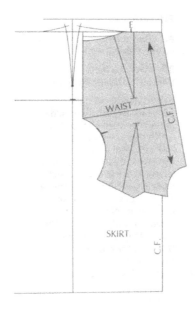

FIGURE 2

A. Match waistlines of skirt and waist drafts from center front to first dartline.

B. On skirt draft, place a dot a *scant* ⅛" (0.32 cm) away from waist dartline measuring towards side seam. Label *E.*

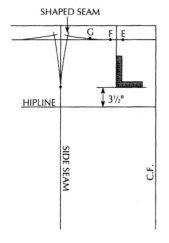

FIGURE 3

A. From E measure over *one-half* of the dart underlay. Dot and label F.

B. Find center between E and F and square a grainline down to dart guideline.

C. On waistline, place a crossmark at center between shaped side seam and F. Dot and label G.

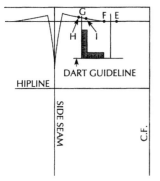

FIGURE 4

A. At G, square a line to dart guideline for center of second dart.

B. At waistline, measure one-half of remaining dart underlay on either side of line G. Dot and label H and I (as illustrated).

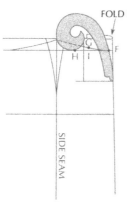

FOLD DART NEAR C.F.

FIGURE 5

A. Crease paper on grainline between E and F.

B. With French curve, draw a curved line from F to dart guideline.

C. Trace this line through to opposite side.

D. Open draft and pencil in traced line. Use French curve for accuracy.

E. Repeat procedure for dart underlay H and I.

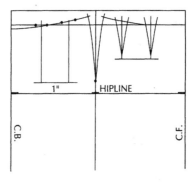

FIGURE 6

A. From back hipline, measure up 1" (2.54 cm) and draw a line parallel to hipline for guide to end of dart.

B. For marking of darts repeat same procedure as for front using skirt back measurements.

SKIRT SLOPER WITH TWO DARTS

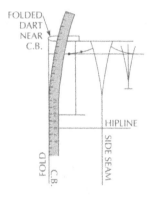

FIGURE 7

To true darts use hip curve ruler.

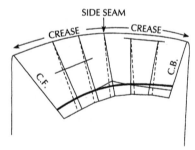

**FIGURE 8,
TRUEING WAISTLINE**

A. For procedure on closing of darts and trueing of waistline, refer to SKIRT SLOPER WITH ONE DART, FIGURE 8, A THROUGH F.

B. Trace new blended waistline through dart underlays.

C. Open draft and pencil in traced line.

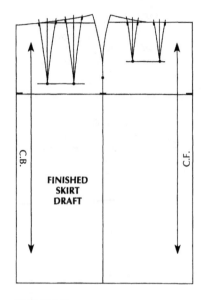

FIGURE 9

To complete skirt sloper with two darts, refer to SKIRT SLOPER WITH ONE DART, FIGURES 9 AND 10.

FITTED TORSO SLOPER WITH DARTS

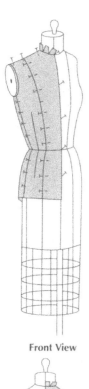

Front View

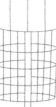

Back View

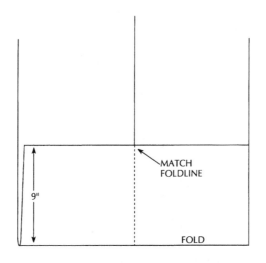

MATCH FOLDLINE

9"

FOLD

WIDTH OF FRONT

C.B.

UNDERARM SEAM GUIDELINE

C.F.

WAISTLINE

7"   7"

HIPLINE

FIGURE 1

A. Cut paper approximately 24" X 30" (60.96 X 76.20 cm).

B. To obtain true right angle lines, fold paper in half lengthwise.

C. Open paper and fold up bottom edge approximately 9" (22.86 cm) matching foldlines.

D. Open paper and draw lines over creases.

FIGURE 2

A. Label *waistline* and *underarm seam guideline* (as illustrated).

B. Measure width of *front waist sloper* at underarm and armhole intersection across to center front.

C. From underarm seam guideline at top and bottom of right side of draft, measure width of front waist sloper. Dot. Draw a line connecting dots. Label *center front*.

D. Establish *center back* following same procedure as for center front.

E. From center front and center back at waistline measure down 7" (17.78 cm). Dot. Draw a line connecting dots and label *hipline*.

FITTED TORSO SLOPER WITH DARTS

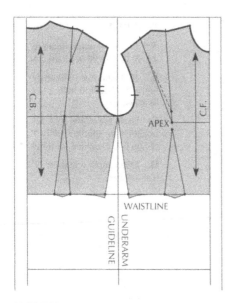

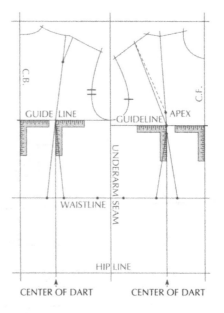

FIGURE 3

A. Place center front of front waist sloper to center front line on draft matching waistlines.

B. Outline armhole, shoulder, and neckline (heavier line). Crossmark armhole, shoulder, and waistline darts. Indicate all dots with awl.

C. Place center back of back waist sloper to center back line of draft matching waistlines. Repeat as for front.

FIGURE 4

A. Remove slopers. Indicate dots with pencil marks and draw dartlines.

B. Square a line from center front through *apex* to underarm.

C. Square a line down from apex to hipline. Line must be parallel to center front. Label *center of dart.* Dart underlay should be balanced on both sides of center line. If uneven, adjust.

D. Square a line down from top of back waistline dart to hipline. Label *center of dart.*

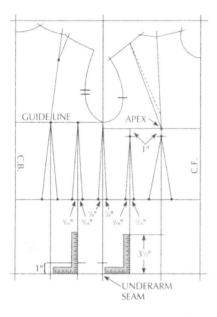

GUIDELINE APEX

C.B.

C.F.

1"

3½"

1"

UNDERARM
SEAM

FIGURE 5

A. To shape underarm seam on waistline, measure ⅝" (1.59 cm) on each side of underarm seam guideline. Dot.

B. Draw a line from dots to armhole intersection.

C. On front waistline, divide area between shaped underarm seam and dartline nearest to underarm seam in half. Dot.

D. Square a line from hipline through dot and up to 1" (2.54 cm) below apex line for center of second front dart.

E. Repeat same for back side dart extending line to back guideline (as illustrated).

Note: The measurements of dart underlays are standard for most industrial model forms. However, when working with other measurements slight adjustments are needed. It may be necessary when fitting a sloper to increase or decrease the dart underlay and shape of underarm seam. Adjustments also depend upon thickness of fabric.

F. To indicate terminating points of hip darts, establish the following dots:

> **1.** 1" (2.54 cm) above hipline on back dartlines and side seam.

> **2.** 3½" (8.89 cm) above hipline on front dartlines.

G. To establish depth of front and back side dart underlays, subtract ⅝" (1.59 cm) from the original underarm shaping at the waistline, which was 1⅜" (3.49 cm). *Example:* 1⅜" (3.49 cm) minus ⅝" (1.59 cm) equals ⅚" (1.91 cm) minus ⅛" (0.32 cm) for ease equals ⅝" (1.59 cm) for each front and back side dart. Measure half of ⅝" (1.59 cm), which is ⁵⁄₁₆" (0.79 cm) on either side of center dartline. Dot.

H. Connect front waistline dots to dot 1" (2.54 cm) below apex guidelines (as illustrated).

I. Connect back waistline dots to guideline (as illustrated).

FITTED TORSO SLOPER WITH DARTS

COMPLETING DARTS ON HIP SECTION OF TORSO

Note: 1. Refer to illustrations for proper placement of ruler and French curve. *2.* Accuracy is *very important.*

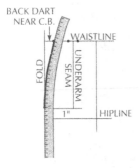

FIGURE 6

Fold back dart nearest center back on center dartline and with hip curve ruler place measurement of 15" (38.10 cm) at 1" (2.54 cm) guideline. Draw a curved dartline. Trace curved line to other side.

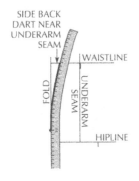

FIGURE 7

Repeat for side back dart, placing measurement of 10" (25.40 cm) at the 1" (2.54 cm) guideline.

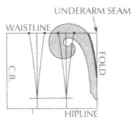

FIGURE 8

Fold on underarm guideline and with French curve, draw a curved seamline ending at 1" (2.54 cm) guideline. Trace curved line to other side.

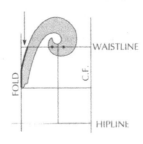

FIGURE 9

For side front dart repeat same as for underarm dart, placing French curve at 3½" (8.89 cm) guideline.

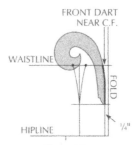

Figure 10

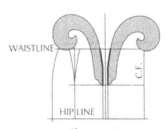

Figure 10A

FIGURES 10 & 10A

Fold front dart on dartline nearest center front. With French curve, draw a curved dartline ending ¼" (0.64 cm) away from fold at 3½" (8.89 cm) guideline. Continue line ¼" (0.64 cm) away from fold down to hipline.

Note: 1. On the average figure, this dart does not end in a point as other darts. However, if figure happens to have a small bust, thick waist, or rounded stomach, dart may end in a point at hipline. Adjustment can be made when testing in muslin. *2.* Figure 10A illustrates trueing of a dart without folding on center line of dart. This method can be applied to all darts if desired.

FITTED TORSO SLOPER WITH DARTS

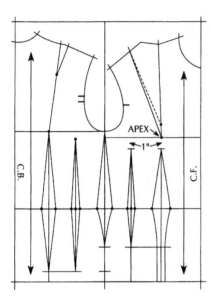

FIGURE 11

A. Establish grainlines parallel to center front and center back.

B. Draft is now ready for testing in muslin. Important points to check are:

  1. Neckline and shoulder intersection (see Figure 17A, page 55).

  2. Shoulder and armhole intersection (see Figure 17B, page 55).

  3. Underarm and armhole

intersection (see Figure 17C, page 55).

C. Transfer corrections, if any, to draft.

D. Copy draft onto oaktag and cut on all finished lines.

E. Notch all crossmarks and dartlines.

F. With awl indicate apex, end of darts, and dart dots at waistline.

Finished Sloper

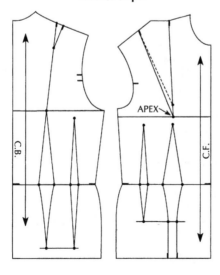

DARTLESS TORSO SLOPER

The dartless sloper can only be used satisfactorily in developing casual and loose-fitting clothing, since the fit across the bustline is sacrificed to a degree when darts are eliminated. The larger the bust, the greater the sacrifice. Therefore, the dartless sloper is recommended for use only when working on small to average sizes with small to average bustline measurements.

Garments best suited to the use of the dartless sloper are shirts, shirtwaist dresses, caftans, kimonos, dolman- and tent-type dresses.

The standard sleeve will fit into this armhole but will have less ease.

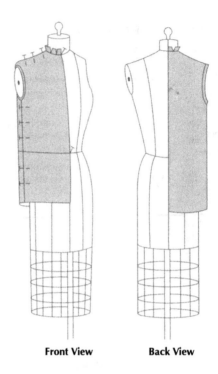

Front View   Back View

PREPARATION OF FRONT WAIST

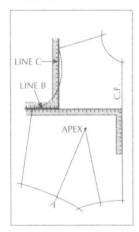

FIGURE 1

A. Cut paper approximately 15" × 20" (38.10 × 50.80 cm).

B. Use *one-dart front waist sloper* and outline. With awl indicate dart and apex.

C. Remove sloper. True all lines, crossing all intersections.

D. Label dartline at waistline *A* (as illustrated).

E. Place L-square to center front touching underarm intersection. Draw a short line from underarm seam (heavier line). Label *line B*.

F. Square a line from line B up to end of shoulder. Label *line C*.

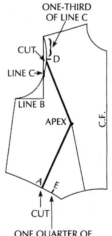

FIGURE 2

A. From end of shoulder measure down one-third of line C. Place a crossmark at armhole. Label *D*.

B. Draw a line from D to apex (heavier line).

C. From waistline A measure one-quarter of dart underlay. Crossmark and label *E*.

D. Accurately cut out waist draft.

E. Cut on lines from A to apex and from D to apex.

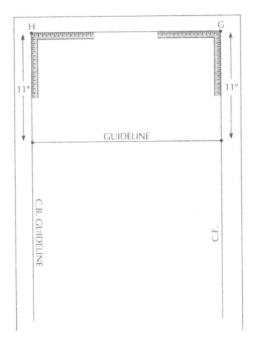

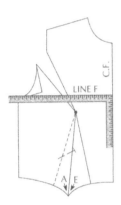

FIGURE 3

A. Decrease waistline dart by matching A to E. Pin.

Note: This will introduce automatically additional fullness to the armhole.

B. Square a new line from center front to underarm intersection. Label *line F.*

DEVELOPMENT OF SLOPER

FIGURE 4

A. Cut another sheet of paper approximately 25" × 35" (63.50 × 88.90 cm).

B. Draw a right angle across top and down at right-hand edge of paper. Label *G* and *center front.*

C. Measure the total width of back waist sloper and adjusted front waist draft from centers to underarm intersections. From G measure over this amount plus 1"

(2.54 cm). Dot. Label *H.* Square a line down paper. Label *CB Guideline.*

Note: Recheck all squared lines for accuracy and to ensure proper fit and balance of sloper.

D. From G and H, measure down 11" (27.94 cm). Dot.

E. Draw a line between dots and label *guideline.*

DARTLESS TORSO SLOPER

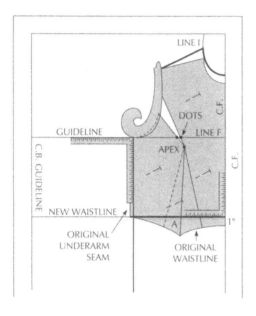

FIGURE 5

A. Match line F and center front of adjusted front waist draft to center front and guideline on paper. Pin.

B. To establish new underarm seam, square a line from guideline down to end of paper.

Note: The original underarm seam at waistline may extend slightly (as illustrated) or may be within the adjusted underarm seam.

C. Place L-square touching center front and bottom of underarm seam. Draw a line to center back. Label *new waistline.*

Note: 1. New waistline will be above original waistline at center

front. How much depends upon sloper used and depth of dart underlay. *2.* If new waistline is more than 1" (2.54 cm) above original waistline, measure up only 1" (2.54 cm) and draw a line across to center back. This line may be slightly below end of underarm.

D. To regain the loss of the center front length, draw a guideline up from neckline and shoulder intersection parallel to center front. Label *line I.*

E. Measure distance between original and new waistline at center front.

F. Measure up this amount at center front of neckline and

shoulder and neckline intersection. Dot.

G. Draw in new shoulderline and new neckline using designer's neckline curve (heavier line).

H. With French curve, blend armhole (as illustrated).

I. Trace armhole and new front waistline. Indicate apex with awl.

J. Dot both sides of spread on *guideline* (as illustrated).

K. Remove draft. True and pencil in traced lines and dots.

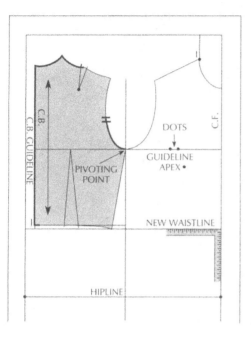

FIGURE 6

A. For hipline, measure down 7" (17.78 cm) from waistline at center front and center back. Dot. Draw a line connecting dots and label *hipline*.

B. To develop back, match underarm of back waist sloper (with shoulder dart) to front underarm. At this point, pivot sloper until center back is parallel with center back guideline.

Note: Back waistline may or may not match new waistline. (Adjustment to shorten back will be made later.)

C. Crossmark center back/waistline intersection. Label *J*.

D. Outline center back, neckline, and shoulder to first dartline. Crossmark at shoulder. Outline lower half of armhole (heavier line).

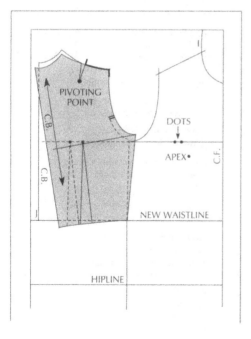

FIGURE 7

A. To eliminate shoulder dart, hold sloper at pivoting point with push pin or pencil point and close dart.

B. Outline remaining shoulder and crossmark armhole (heavier line).

DARTLESS TORSO SLOPER

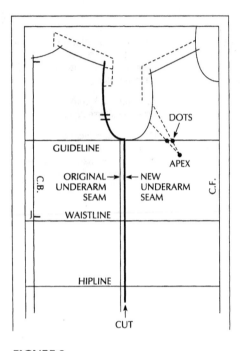

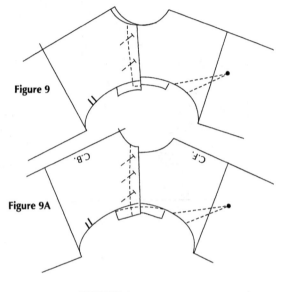

Figure 9

Figure 9A

FIGURE 8

A. Remove sloper and extend center back line to hipline. Using French curve, blend back armhole (heavier line). True all lines, crossing all intersections.

B. At center back, measure distance between crossmark J and waistline. Measure down this amount from center back neckline intersection and crossmark.

Note: The dart fullness added at the front armhole has moved the underarm seam automatically towards the back, which must be adjusted or sleeve when set-in

will swing towards the back. To adjust: *1.* Measure the distance between the two dots on front guideline. *2.* Measure this amount from original underarm seam toward center front. Draw a line parallel to original underarm seam (heavier line). Label *new underarm seam.*

C. Accurately cut out slopers on finished lines with *one exception:* allow approximately 1" (2.54 cm) for trueing front shoulder and front and back armholes (broken line).

FIGURE 9

A. To true neckline, shoulder, and armhole intersection, match back shoulderline to front shoulderline. Pin.

B. From crossmark at center back, blend new neckline to shoulder to nothing on front neckline (heavier line). While in pinned position, cut neckline.

C. Pin and match front and back armholes (Figure 9A).

Note: This retains the ¼" (0.64 cm) back shoulder ease.

Blend shoulder and armhole intersection (broken line).

D. Seperate and cut front shoulder and blended front and back armholes. (Figure 9A).

Note: Recheck underarm seam. Pin together starting at waistline. Adjust at armhole and hipline. Hipline must be on crosswise grainline.

E. Cut out remaining sloper.

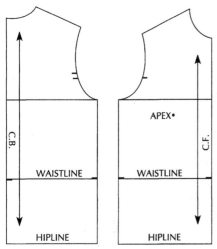

Finished Sloper

FIGURE 10

A. Establish grainlines parallel to center front and center back.

B. To establish armhole crossmark on front, refer to ESTABLISHING SLEEVE CROSSMARKS ON WAIST ARMHOLES.

C. Draft is now ready for testing in muslin. Important points to check are:

> **1.** Neckline and shoulder intersection (see Figure 17A, page 55).
>
> **2.** Underarm and armhole intersection (see Figure 17C, page 55).

D. Transfer corrections, if any, to draft.

E. Copy draft onto oaktag and cut on all finished lines.

F. Notch all crossmarks and dartlines.

G. With awl indicate apex.

FITTED DRESS SLOPER WITHOUT WAISTLINE

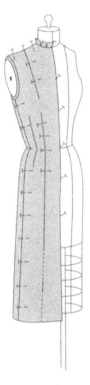

Front View   **Back View**

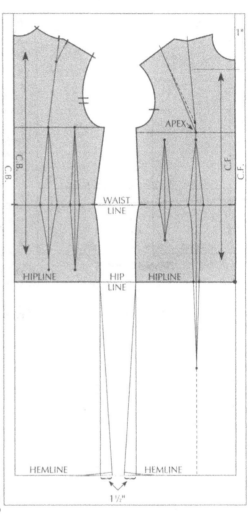

FIGURE 1

A. Cut paper 27" × 52" (68.59 × 132.08 cm).

B. On right-hand side of paper, allow 1" (2.54 cm) and draw a line extending the full length of paper. Label *center front*.

C. Measure length of torso sloper from front neckline and shoulder intersection to hipline. On paper, measure this amount plus 2" (5.08 cm) down on center front. Dot and square a line across paper. Label *hipline*.

D. Measure distance between hipline and waistline on sloper. From hipline dot, measure up this amount and square a line across paper. Label *waistline*.

E. Allow enough room for placing slopers and shaping side seams at hemline, draw a line on left-hand side of paper parallel to center front. Label *center back*.

F. Place front and back torso sloper on paper matching centers, waistline, and hipline.

G. Outline sloper (heavier line). Crossmark armholes and shoulder darts. With awl indicate dots at apex, end and depth of darts (as illustrated).

FITTED DRESS SLOPER WITHOUT WAISTLINE

H. Remove sloper and draw in darts. True all lines, crossing all intersections.

I. From waistline at center front measure length of skirt desired and dot. Square a line across paper. Label *hemline.*

J. Extend side seams to hemline parallel to center front and back.

K. At hemline and side seam intersection, measure over 1" (2.54 cm). Dot. Draw new side seam lines from dots ending between hipline and waistline. Shape at waistline as illustrated.

Note: The 1" (2.54 cm) seam shaping at the hemline is for a 28" (71.12 cm) skirt length. For a longer skirt, extend the line. The line will widen automatically as the skirt is lengthened and will become narrower as the skirt is shortened.

L. Dart nearest center front should be extended below hipline approximately 9" to 10" (22.86 – 25.40 cm) and tapered to a point.

Note: Dart may be tapered down to hemline giving sloper a panelled effect (broken line).

M. Establish grainlines parallel to center front and center back.

N. Draft is now ready to be tested in muslin.

FINISHED SLOPER

Note: For a semi-fitted dress sloper side darts can be eliminated.

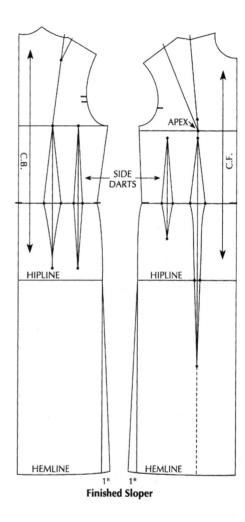

Finished Sloper

PRINCESS LINE DRESS SLOPER

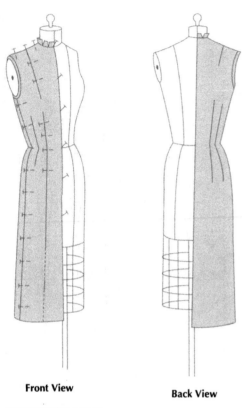

Front View

Back View

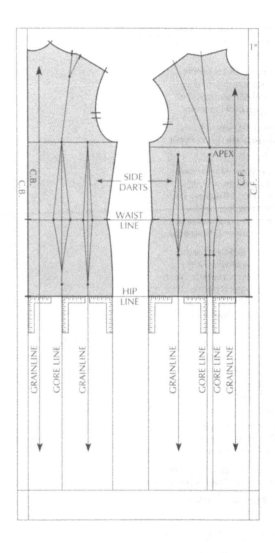

PRINCESS LINE DRESS SLOPER

FIGURE 1

A. To develop princess line dress sloper follow instructions for Fitted Dress Sloper without Waistline, Figure 1, A through J.

B. To establish gore lines and side grainlines, draw lines down from end of darts parallel to center front and center back.

C. Extend center front and center back grainlines as illustrated.

D. Label gore line and grainlines as illustrated.

Figure 2

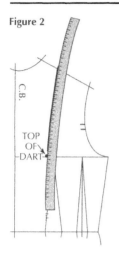

C.B.

TOP
OF
DART

Figure 2A   **Figure 2B**

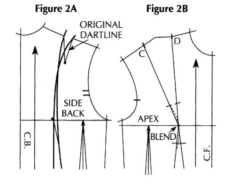

ORIGINAL
DARTLINE

SIDE
BACK

C.B.

C
D

APEX

BLEND

C.F.

FINISHED SLOPER

Note: For a semi-fitted princess line sloper, side darts may be eliminated.

FIGURE 2

A.   To develop princess line on back waist section, place curved ruler approximately 2" to 3" (5.08 to 7.62 cm) above waistline touching shoulder and top of dart crossmark nearest neckline.

B.   Draw a slightly curved line to top of waistline dart (heavier line).

C.   To adjust side back dartline, blend with a slightly curved line other shoulder dart crossmark to below end of original shoulder dart (as illustrated, Figure 2A).

D.   To adjust apex area, blend as illustrated (broken line, Figure 2B).

E.   To shape all skirt seams, measure out 1" (2.54 cm) and blend (as illustrated).

Note: The 1" (2.54 cm) seam shaping is for a 28" (71.12 cm) skirt length. For a longer skirt, extend the line. The line will automatically widen as skirt is lengthened and will become narrower as the skirt is shortened.

F.   Establish crossmarks on all seams (as illustrated).

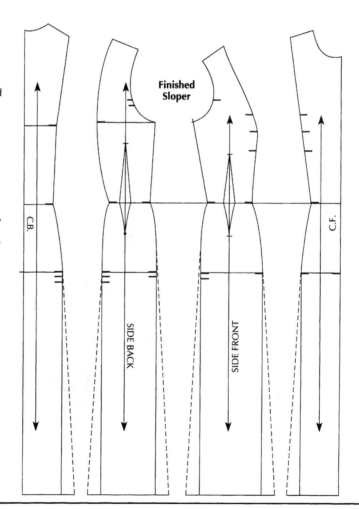

Finished Sloper

C.B.

C.F.

SIDE BACK

SIDE FRONT

SHIFT SLOPER WITH SHOULDER DART

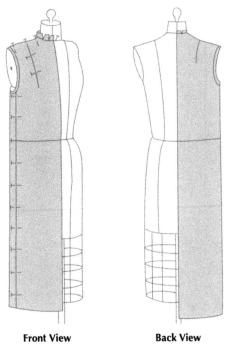

Front View   **Back View**

The shift sloper is developed with balanced seams and, therefore, can be used to develop garments made in stripes, plaids, and checks.

PREPARATION OF SLOPERS

FIGURE 1

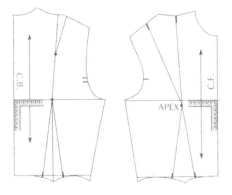

A. Use *front and back waist slopers with shoulder and waistline darts.*

B. On front and back slopers (if missing), square a line from center front and center back of waist to intersection at armhole and underarm. (This is the widest width of front and back slopers.)

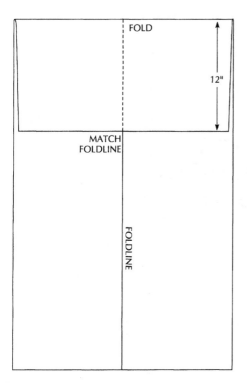

FIGURE 2

A. Cut paper approximately 24" × 45" (60.96 × 114.30 cm) or longer if desired.

B. To obtain true right-angle lines, fold paper in half lengthwise.

C. Open paper and fold down end of paper approximately 12" (30.48 cm) matching foldline.

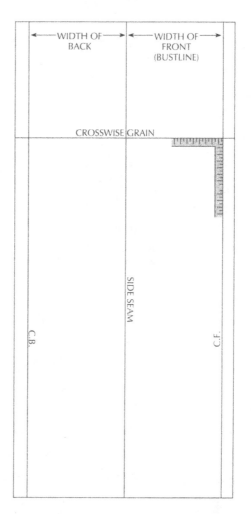

FIGURE 3

A. Open paper and draw lines over creases. Label *lines as illustrated.*

B. From side seam on right-hand side of paper, at top and bottom of draft, measure widest

width of front sloper. Dot. Draw a line between dots and label *center front.*

C. Repeat for back, using widest width of back sloper. Label *center back.*

SHIFT SLOPER WITH SHOULDER DART

FIGURE 4

A. Place front waist sloper on draft matching underarm intersection and center front of sloper to crosswise grainline and center front of paper (as illustrated).

B. Outline armhole and crossmarks, shoulder, crossmark shoulder dart, neckline, and crossmark at waistline and center front intersection (heavier line). With awl indicate apex.

C. Repeat for back with *one exception:* do not indicate waistline.

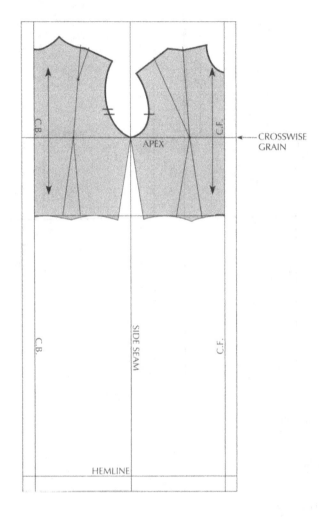

SHIFT SLOPER WITH SHOULDER DART

FIGURE 5

A. Remove slopers. Square a line from center front and waistline crossmark to center back. Line must be parallel to crosswise grainline. Label *waistline* and crossmark at center back.

B. From waistline at center front, measure down length desired. Dot. Square a line to center back and label *hemline.*

C. Cup and close front and back shoulder darts before trueing shoulderlines. Refer to TWO-DART FRONT AND BACK WAIST SLOPER for trueing:

> **1.** Front shoulder dart, see Figure 7, A to C.

> **2.** Back shoulder dart, see Figure 13, A to E.

D. Cut excess paper from all seamlines.

Note: 1. If desired, shift may be developed without a side seam and cut as follows:

• Center front on fold with seam at center back

• Center back on fold with seam at center front

• Seams at both center front and center back

2. For design variations, front shoulder dart may be pivoted many positions. Refer to DESIGNING APPAREL THROUGH THE FLAT PATTERN, 6th EDITION.

E. Establish grainlines parallel to center front and center back.

F. Draft is now ready to be tested in muslin.

G. Transfer corrections, if any, to draft.

H. Copy draft in oaktag and cut on all finished lines.

I. Notch all crossmarks and dartlines.

J. With awl indicate end of darts.

SHIFT SLOPER WITH SHOULDER DART

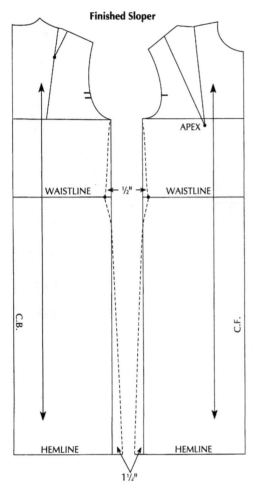

Finished Sloper

APEX

WAISTLINE ←— ½" —→ WAISTLINE

C.B.

C.F.

HEMLINE   HEMLINE

1½"

FIGURE 6,
FINISHED SLOPER

Note: 1. If desired, slight additional width may be added at hemline and slight shaping may be used at waistline when cutting shift with a side seam (as illustrated). *2.* The 1½" (3.81 cm) flare at hemline is for a 28" (71.12 cm) skirt length. For a longer skirt, extend the line. The flare will widen automatically as the skirt is lengthened and will become narrower as the skirt is shortened.

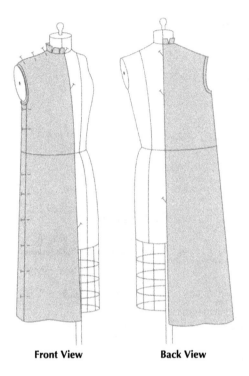

Front View   **Back View**

The tent silhouette sloper is developed as a waist sloper and full-length dress sloper with balanced seams. Therefore, it can be used to develop garments made in stripe, check or plaid fabric.

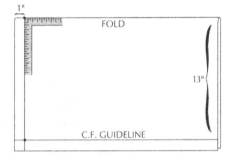

WAIST SLOPER

FIGURE 1

A. Cut paper approximately 22" (55.88 cm) square. Fold paper in half.

B. With fold of paper away from you, square a line 13" (33.02 cm) long on the left-hand side of the paper. Allow approximately 1" (2.54 cm) margin from paper edge. Dot.

C. Measure 13" (33.02 cm) at right-hand edge of paper. Dot.

D. Draw a line connecting dots. Label *center front guideline.* With awl transfer dots to opposite side of paper.

TENT SLOPER

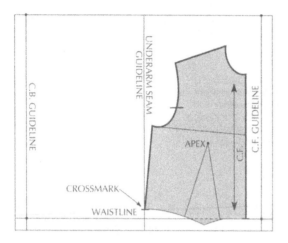

FIGURE 2

A. Open draft. Draw a line connecting dots. Label *center back* and *waistline* (as illustrated).

B. Draw a line over crease. Label *underarm seam guideline.*

C. Use *one-dart front waist sloper.* Match center front waistline intersection of sloper to waistline on paper with:

    1. underarm and waistline intersection touching underarm seam guideline;

    2. center front of sloper parallel to center front on paper.

D. Outline center front, neckline, shoulder, armhole, armhole crossmark, and underarm seam. Add crossmarks at waistline (heavier line).

E. Indicate apex with awl.

FIGURE 3

A. Remove sloper. True all lines, crossing all intersections.

B. Square a line from center front through and beyond underarm and armhole intersection.

C. Measure, on this line, the distance from front underarm and armhole intersection to underarm seam guideline. Measure this amount on opposite side from underarm seam guideline to determine placement of back sloper. Dot.

Note: If a tent silhouette with fullness directed towards center back is desired, use *back waist sloper with neckline dart* (follow same instructions as below).

D. Label *back sloper with shoulder dart A, B, C* (as illustrated).

E. Place sloper with C touching dot and underarm touching waistline crossmark.

F. Outline underarm seam, armhole, armhole crossmarks, and shoulder to B (heavier line). Crossmark.

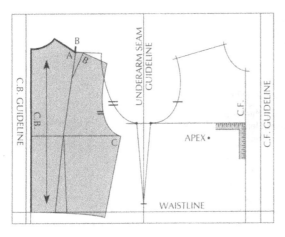

FIGURE 4

A. To close shoulder or neckline dart, lift sloper and match A to crossmark B. From this point, pivot sloper until center back is parallel to center back guideline.

B. Outline center back, neckline, and shoulder to A (heavier line).

Note: For *back waist with neckline dart,* outline center back and neckline to A.

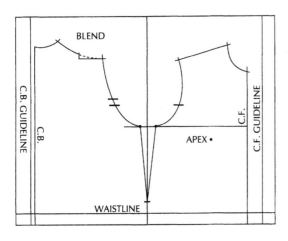

FIGURE 5

A. Remove sloper. True all lines, crossing all intersections. Blend shoulder (broken line).

B. Draft is now ready for testing in muslin.

C. Transfer corrections, if any, to draft.

D. Copy draft onto oaktag. Cut on all finished lines and notch crossmarks.

TENT SLOPER

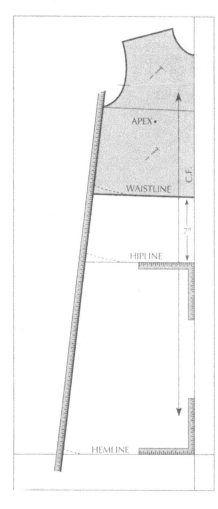

APEX •

C.F.

WAISTLINE

7"

HIPLINE

HEMLINE

FULL-LENGTH DRESS SLOPER

FIGURE 6

A.   Cut paper approximately 17" X 48" (43.18 X 121.92 cm).

B.   Draw a line at right-hand edge of paper the full length of paper. Label *center front*.

C.   Place and pin front tent waist sloper to paper (as illustrated).

D.   Outline waistline, neckline, shoulder, and armhole to underarm. Indicate apex dot and armhole crossmark (heavier line). Remove sloper.

E.   From waistline at center front, measure down length desired. Dot. Square a line across paper. Label *hemline*.

F.   Place yardstick at underarm (as illustrated) and extend seamline down to hemline.

G.   From waistline at center front measure down 7" (17.78 cm) and dot. Square a line across paper. Label *hipline*.

H.   To obtain correct shaping at underarm of waistline, measure distance between line above apex and waistline at center front.

I.   Measure this amount at underarm. Dot. Blend a slightly curved line into waistline (broken line).

J.   Repeat for hipline and hemline (broken line).

K.   Repeat same for back.

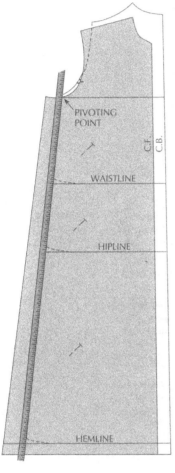

FIGURE 7

A. To complete sloper allow 1" (2.54 cm) seams at underarm and hemline.

B. Match underarm seams, with front face up, at underarm/armhole intersection and pivot front from this point until center front is parallel to center back. Pin securely to prevent shifting when trueing underarm seam.

Note: If underarm seams *do not match,* redraw seam and compromise the difference.

C. While in pinned position, cut on underarm seamline and notch adjusted waistline and hipline.

D. Check hemline and adjust, if necessary, by compromising. Cut excess paper from hemline.

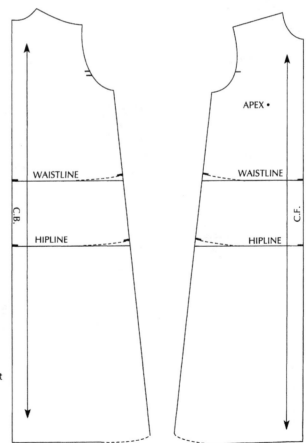

FIGURE 8

A. Separate draft. Establish grainlines parallel to center front and center back.

B. Copy draft onto oaktag.

C. Cut on finished lines and notch crossmarks.

CAPE SLOPER

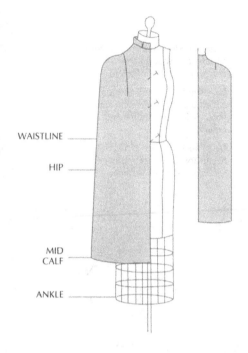

WAISTLINE

HIP

MID
CALF

ANKLE

FIGURE 1

A. Cut paper approximately 40" × 50" (101.60 × 127.00 cm) for mid-calf length.

B. Fold paper in half as illustrated. Label *fold* and at right end of fold *A*.

C. From A measure from fold towards edge of paper 19" (48.26 cm). Dot. Repeat this measurement at left edge of fold. Dot. Connect dots. Label *center front*.

D. From A measure over on fold 12" (30.48 cm). Dot. Square a line from dot through center front. Label *guideline*.

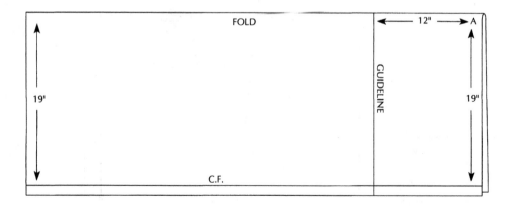

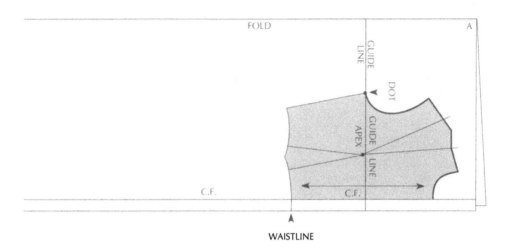

FOLD   A

GUIDE LINE

DOT

GUIDE LINE

APEX

GUIDE LINE

C.F.   C.F.

WAISTLINE

FIGURE 2

A. On two-dart front sloper, square a line from center front of waist to intersection at underarm and armhole. Label *guideline.*

Note: If there is a corresponding line on the sloper, eliminate this step.

B. Place center front of sloper to center front of paper matching guideline on sloper to guideline on paper.

C. Outline neck, shoulder, shoulder dart crossmarks and armhole (heavier line). Dot underarm intersection. With awl indicate apex and crossmark center front at waistline. Label *waistline.*

CAPE SLOPER

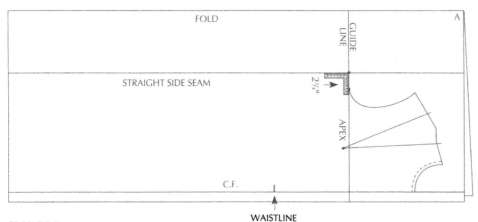

FIGURE 3

A. Remove sloper, draw in shoulder dart.

B. Measure biceps of sleeve sloper.

C. Subtract 2¼" (5.72 cm). (This eliminates the 2" (5.08 cm) ease allowance of sleeve plus ¼" (0.64 cm.)

D. Divide the remaining measurement into four parts.
Example: Biceps measurement
for size 12 sleeve = 13"   (33.02 cm)
      Minus   2¼" (5.75 cm)
                 10¾" (27.31 cm)
Divide by 4   = 2¹¹⁄₁₆" (6.82 cm)
Round out measurement to 2¾" (6.99 cm).

E. Measure from dot at armhole intersection 2¾" (6.99 cm) towards fold. Dot.

F. From dot square a line above and below guideline. Label *straight side seam.*

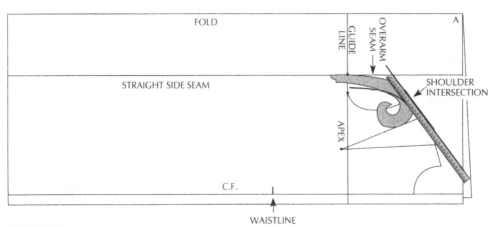

FIGURE 4

A. Balance ruler on shoulderline (as illustrated).

B. Extend shoulderline to intersect straight side seam (heavier line).

C. To shape overarm, place and move French curve into position touching end of shoulder and side seam and guideline

intersection. Draw curved overarm seamline (heavier line). Label *overarm seam.*

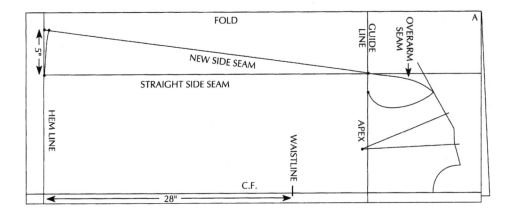

FIGURE 5

A. From waistline crossmark at center front, measure across desired length. Dot. Illustrated mid-calf length, 28" (71.12 cm). Square a line to fold. Label *hemline* and dot hemline at center front and straight side seam intersection.

B. From dot at side seam, measure towards fold 5" (12.70 cm). Dot. Connect dot to guideline. Label *new side seam.*

C. To shape hemline at new side seam, measure length of straight side seamline from guideline to hemline. Repeat this amount on new side seam. Dot. Curve hemline as illustrated.

CAPE SLOPER

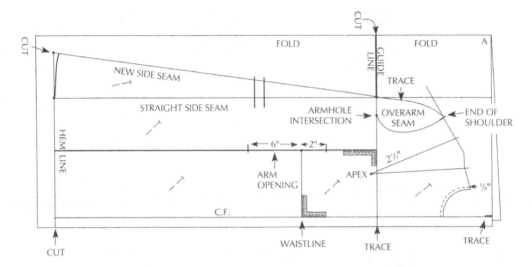

FIGURE 6

A. To establish arm opening, measure from apex on guideline towards straight side seam 2½" (6.35 cm). Dot. Square a line from dot down to hemline.

B. Square a line across from waistline crossmark to this line. Dot.

C. From dot measure up 2" (5.08 cm) and down 6" (15.24 cm). Crossmark and label *arm opening.*

Note: This arm opening is the standard position, however it may be placed where desired or eliminated completely.

D. Crossmark new side seam as illustrated intersecting straight side seam.

E. Pin draft. Trace to opposite side straight side seam, all crossmarks, overarm seam to end of shoulder and guideline across to center front. Trace a short line

at top and bottom of center front line. With awl indicate dot at armhole intersection.

F. Cut excess paper from hemline and new side seam and on guideline to fold (heavier line).

G. Lower neckline ⅛" to ¼" (0.32 to 0.64 cm) (broken line). Illustrated: ⅛" (0.32 cm). Repeat seam at back neckline (Figure 7).

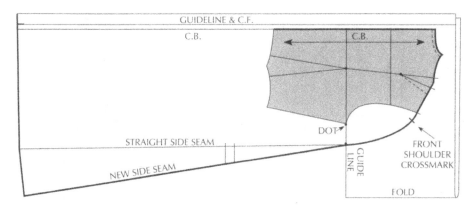

FIGURE 7

A. To develop back, turn paper and work with fold towards you. Pencil in all traced lines, crossmarks and dots. Connect top and bottom traced crossmark from center front. Label line *guideline.*

B. Place armhole and underarm intersection of back sloper to dot on guideline with center back parallel to guideline on draft.

Note: Center back of sloper may or may not touch guideline on draft.

C. Outline shoulder, neckline and center back of sloper and crossmark shoulder dartlines, and end of shoulder (heavier lines). With awl indicate end of shoulder dart.

D. Remove sloper, draw in shoulder dart and extend center back line to hemline. Label *center back.*

E. Pencil in blank space from shoulder to overarm seamline (additional back shoulder ease).

Note: Original waist slopers may

be incorrect or back shoulder blade area may be rounder than the average figure, if space extends 1¼" (3.18 cm). To correct, move shoulder dartline ⅛" (0.32 cm) towards armhole (broken line) to help ease in additional shoulder length obtained on back shoulder. Balance remaining ease on either side of dart. All ease must be retained within the shoulder area as sloper is balanced for stripes, checks, and plaids. Final adjustment should be made when testing sloper in muslin.

CAPE SLOPER

FIGURE 8

A. Separate draft. Establish grainlines parallel to center front and center back as illustrated.

B. Draft is now ready to be tested in muslin.

C. Transfer corrections to draft, and copy draft onto oaktag. Cut on all finished lines.

D. Notch all crossmarks and dartlines.

E. With awl indicate apex and end of darts.

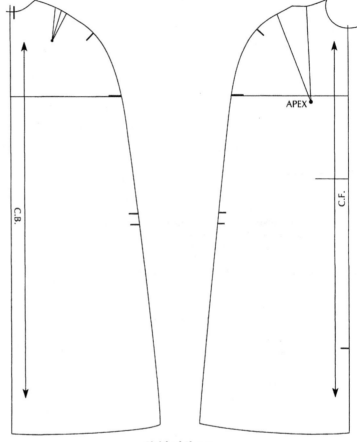

Finished Sloper

CAFTAN SLOPER
(WITH AND WITHOUT SHOULDER DARTS)

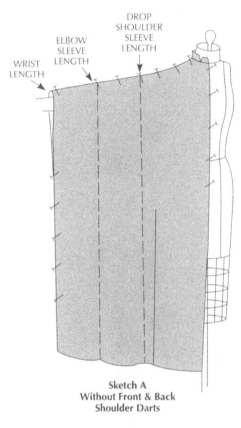

WRIST LENGTH

ELBOW SLEEVE LENGTH

DROP SHOULDER SLEEVE LENGTH

Sketch A
Without Front & Back
Shoulder Darts

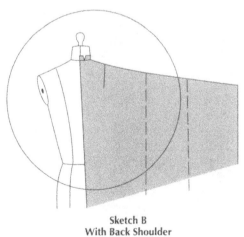

Sketch B
With Back Shoulder
Dart

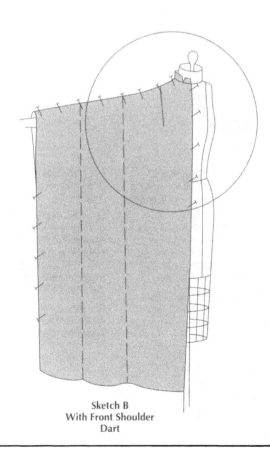

Sketch B
With Front Shoulder
Dart

CAFTAN SLOPER
(WITHOUT SHOULDER DARTS)

Figure 1

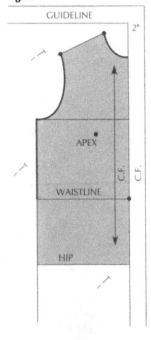

Figure 1A

SKETCH A

FIGURE 1

A. Cut two sheets of paper approximately 40" X 62" (101.50 X 157.48 cm) for an ankle length caftan sloper.

B. Pin sheets together and draw a right angle at top and 2" (5.08 cm) in from the *right* edge of the paper. Label *center front* and *guideline* as illustrated.

Note: Use dartless sloper. Refer to Dartless Torso Sloper, pages 80 - 85.

C. Match center front of dartless sloper to center front line on draft.

D. With the exception of the shoulderline, outline sloper as illustrated (heavier line). Dot shoulder at neckline and armhole intersection, waistline on center front and apex. Remove sloper.

E. Square a line across from center front waistline dot. Label *waistline* (Figure 1A).

Figure 2

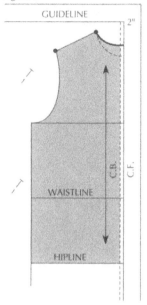

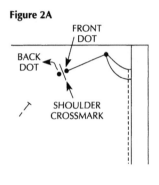

Figure 2A

FIGURE 2

A. Match neckline and shoulder intersection of back dartless sloper to front neck dot on draft. Pivot sloper from this point until center back is parallel to center front on draft. Draw in center back (broken line).

Note: Depending upon sloper, center back may or may not touch center front.

B. Outline back neckline (heavier line) and dot end of shoulder.

C. Remove sloper and establish new end of shoulderline with crossmark between front and back shoulder dots (Figure 2B).

Note: Back shoulderline with or without shoulder dart has ease allowance of ⅛" to ¼" (0.32 to 0.64 cm). This allowance causes the dot on the back shoulder to extend beyond the dot on the front shoulder.

CAFTAN SLOPER
(WITHOUT SHOULDER DARTS)

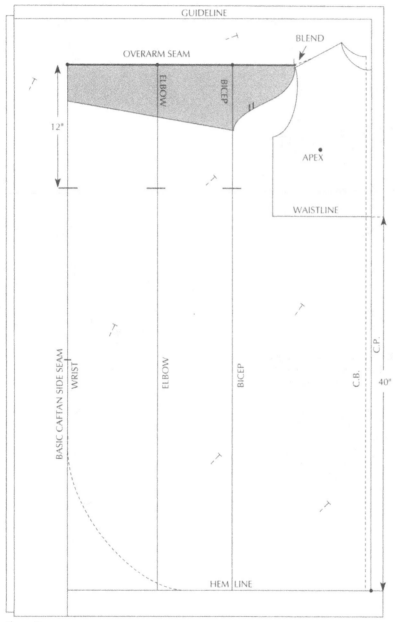

Figure 3

FIGURE 3

A. To establish skirt hemline, measure down from waistline desired length. Dot. Square a line across draft. Label *hemline*. Illustrated: 40" (101.60 cm). Continue broken line for center back.

B. To develop sleeve area for basic caftan, place top of folded straight sleeve sloper to end of shoulder and pivot sleeve until fold of sleeve is parallel to guideline.

C. Outline fold of sleeve (heavier line). Dot end of wrist, elbow and biceps. Label *overarm seam* and remove sloper.

D. From dot at wrist, draw a line down through hemline parallel to center front. Label *caftan side seam*.

E. Establish crossmark for wrist opening as desired on caftan side seam. Illustrated 12" (30.48 cm) down.

Note: Indicate lines for various sleeve lengths and sleeve openings on basic caftan sloper as follows: *1.* Elbow sleeve length – Square a line from overarm seam at elbow down to hemline. *2.* Drop shoulder sleeve length – Square a line from overarm seam at biceps down to hemline. *3.* For depth of sleeve openings repeat wrist opening measurement 12" (30.40 cm) on elbow and biceps line. Crossmark. Place another crossmark on side back (as illustrated).

F. Blend at end of shoulder (broken line) and crossmark as illustrated.

Note: If desired the side seam and hemline intersection may be rounded as illustrated by broken line forming a side slit.

G. Trace through center back (broken line), back neckline, adjusted shoulder, shoulder crossmark, overarm, caftan side seam, elbow line and biceps line, crossmarks, hemline and waistline to opposite side.

CAFTAN SLOPER
(WITHOUT SHOULDER DARTS)

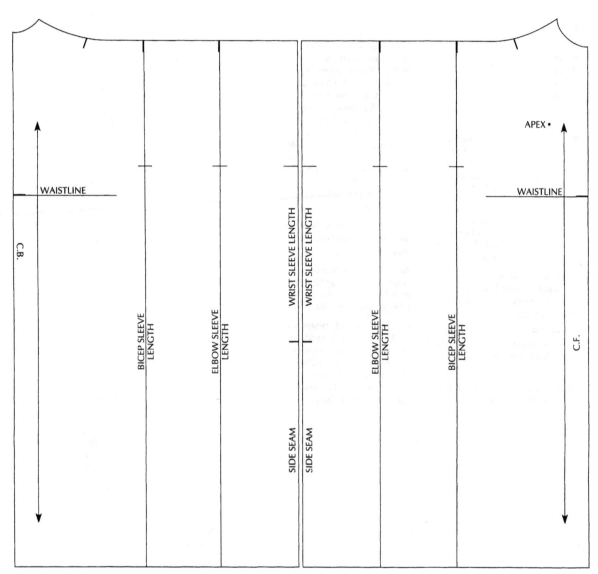

Figure 4 Finished Sloper

FIGURE 4

A. Cut on following finished lines: hemline, straight side seam, overarm seam to dot at neck and shoulder intersection.

B. Notch all crossmarks and dots on overarm seam.

C. To complete sloper separate draft and cut on back and front necklines and center front and center back lines.

D. Draw in all traced lines and notch waistline at center front and center back.

E. Draw in grainline parallel to center front and center back. Label caftan sleeve lengths as illustrated.

F. Draft is now ready to be tested in muslin.

G. Transfer corrections, if any, to draft and copy draft onto oaktag. Cut on all finished lines.

H. Notch all crossmarks and dartlines.

I. With awl indicate apex.

CAFTAN SLOPER
(WITH SHOULDER DARTS)

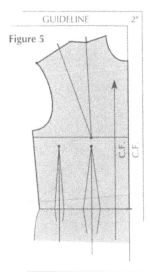

Figure 5

GUIDELINE   2"

C.F.   C.F.

SKETCH B

FIGURE 5

A. Cut two sheets of paper approximately 40" X 62" (101.60 X 157.48 cm) for ankle length caftan sloper.

B. Match center front of torso sloper to center front on paper as illustrated.

C. Outline complete front sloper to waistline. Add dot at end of shoulder, crossmark waistline at center front, indicate shoulder dart with crossmarks and end of dart with awl.

D. Remove sloper. Draw in dart and square a line from waistline crossmark to side seam. Label *waistline*. (Figure 5A).

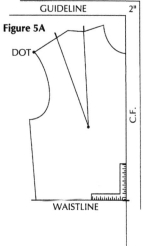

GUIDELINE   2"

Figure 5A

DOT

C.F.

WAISTLINE

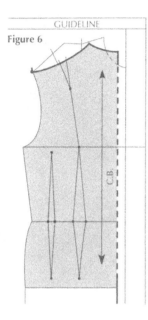

FIGURE 6

A. Match shoulder and armhole intersection of back torso sloper to front shoulder. Hold in position and pivot back until it is parallel to center front.

B. Outline shoulder and neckline (heavier lines). Add crossmarks at end of shoulder and shoulder dart. With awl indicate end of dart. Draw in center back (broken line).

C. Remove sloper. To complete sloper follow instructions for Figures 3 and 4.

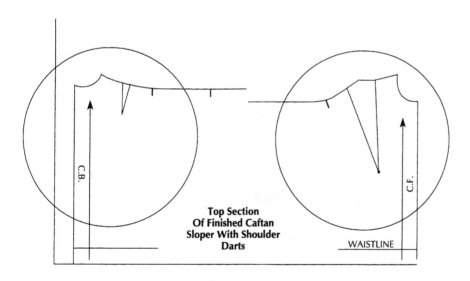

**Top Section
Of Finished Caftan
Sloper With Shoulder
Darts**

WAISTLINE

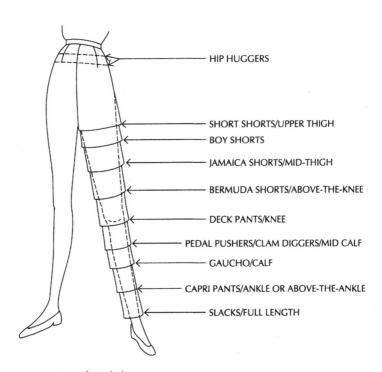

HIP HUGGERS

SHORT SHORTS/UPPER THIGH
BOY SHORTS
JAMAICA SHORTS/MID-THIGH

BERMUDA SHORTS/ABOVE-THE-KNEE

DECK PANTS/KNEE

PEDAL PUSHERS/CLAM DIGGERS/MID CALF

GAUCHO/CALF

CAPRI PANTS/ANKLE OR ABOVE-THE-ANKLE

SLACKS/FULL LENGTH

Pants Length Variations

SLACK SLOPER DEVELOPED FROM SKIRT SLOPER

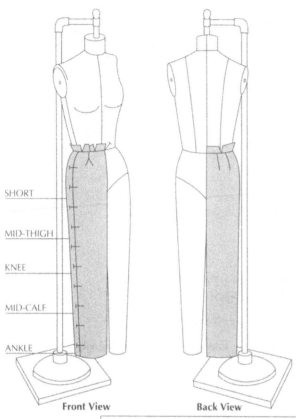

SHORT

MID-THIGH

KNEE

MID-CALF

ANKLE

Front View   Back View

Slacks may be developed from a one- or two-dart skirt sloper. If only a one-dart skirt sloper is available, to develop back darts refer to SKIRT SLOPER WITH TWO DARTS instead of following the instructions given in Figure 4, A through I.

Since all seams on finished slopers are balanced, slopers may be used for stripes, checks, and plaids.

FIGURE 1

A. Cut paper approximately 34" × 45" (86.36 × 114.30 cm).

B. Fold paper in half lengthwise. Open paper and draw a line over crease. Label *side seam.*

C. Measure down from right-hand edge of paper, on side seam, 10" (25.40 cm). Dot and square a line across paper. Label *hipline.*

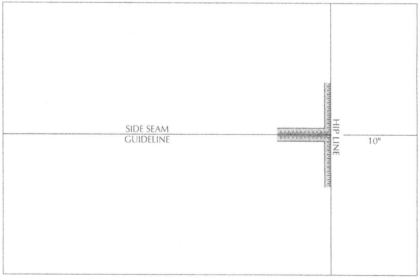

SIDE SEAM
GUIDELINE   HIP LINE   10"

Figure 2

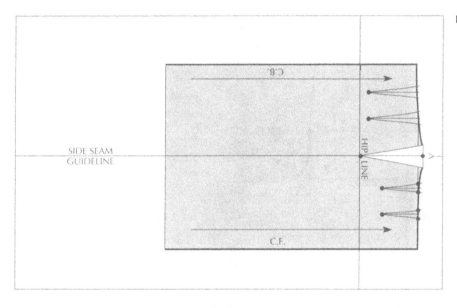

FIGURE 2

A. Place front and back two-dart skirt slopers on paper matching hiplines and side seams.

B. Outline center front, center back, and waistlines, and indicate front waistline darts with dots (heavier lines) and end of darts with awl.

C. Dot at waistline and side seam intersections. Draw a straight line connecting dots. Place a dot at center of line. Label *A* (as illustrated).

D. Remove sloper (Figure 2A). Square a line from center front and waistline intersection across paper parallel to hipline. Label *waistline*.

E. Draw in front darts using French curve as illustrated for side seam in Figure 3A.

Figure 2A

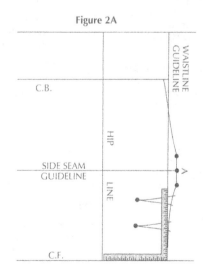

SLACK SLOPER DEVELOPED FROM SKIRT SLOPER

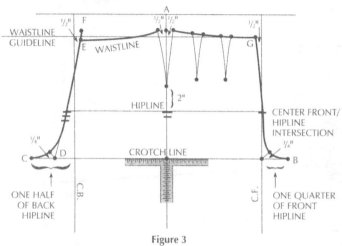

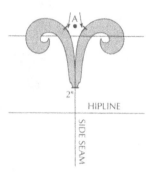

Figure 3

FIGURE 3

A. From dot A, measure down on side seam the crotch depth. Dot. Crotch measurements should include 1" to 2½" (2.54 to 6.35 cm) for ease. The more ease allowed, the lower and looser the crotch line.

Note: If working with slack form measurements, 1¼" (3.18 cm) ease has already been included. Add or subtract from measurement to obtain ease desired.

B. Square a line across paper from side seam on each side of dot. Label *crotch line.* Line should be parallel to hipline.

C. From center front, measure out on crotch line one-quarter of front hipline measurement. Dot and label *B.* For tighter fitting slacks, extend crotch line one-fifth for front.

D. From center back, measure out on crotch line one-half of back hipline measurement. Dot and label *C.* For tighter fitting slacks, extend crotch line two-fifths for back.

E. Divide measurement between C and center back. Dot and label *D.*

F. From center back on waistline, measure in ½" (1.27 cm). Dot and label *E.*

G. Draw a line from D through E.

H. From intersection at D, draw a line ¾" (1.91 cm) on a 45° angle. Dot.

I. Blend a curved line from C through dot to hipline (heavier line).

J. On waistline, measure in ½" (1.27 cm) from center front. Dot and label *G.*

K. Draw a straight line from G to center front and hipline intersection (heavier line).

L. From intersection at center front and crotch line, draw a line ¾" (1.91 cm) on a 45° angle. Dot.

M. Blend a curved line from B through dot to hipline.

N. Add crossmarks on hipline starting with one at center front, two at side seam, and three at center back.

Note: Distances between crossmarks should be ½" (1.27 cm).

O. To shape side seam to hipline, measure in at waistline ½" (1.27 cm) on either side of A. Crossmark.

P. With French curve, draw a line connecting crossmark to hipline, ending approximately 2" to 3" (5.08 to 7.62 cm) above hipline. See *Figure 3A.*

Q. Adjust waistline at new side seam.

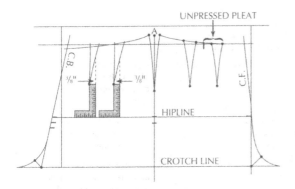

FIGURE 4, DEVELOPING DARTS

A. To determine underlay of back waistline darts, measure waistline of back skirt sloper (*do not* include dart underlay) and waistline of back slacks draft. The difference between the two measurements is for dart underlay.

B. To position back darts, measure distance from center back to first dartline on skirt sloper and repeat on slacks draft. Crossmark.

C. From crossmark measure one-half of dart underlay measurement. Crossmark.

D. From second crossmark measure same amount as between darts on skirt. Crossmark.

E. From third crossmark measure remainder of dart underlay.

F. Square a straight line from hipline through center of each dart underlay (broken line).

Note: Direction of back darts should be in harmony with center back seam rather than side seam (as illustrated).

G. At end of desired length of dart (4" [10.16 cm]), on draft, measure from broken line towards center back ⅜" (0.95 cm). Dot. Draw in darts.

H. Close darts and side seam, and blend waistline. Refer to Skirt Sloper with One Dart, Figure 8, A through F.

I. Trace through dart underlays. Open draft and pencil in traced lines.

Note: Front slack darts may be developed as pleats if desired. To position pleat: 1) measure underlay of both darts, 2) place crossmarks (as illustrated).

SLACK SLOPER DEVELOPED FROM SKIRT SLOPER

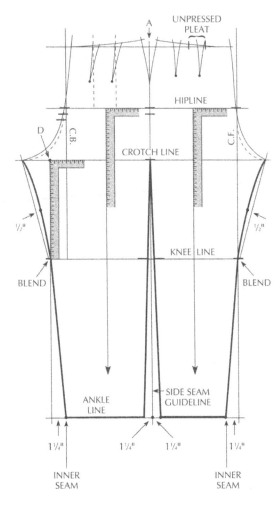

FIGURE 5, DEVELOPING LEG SECTION OF SLACKS

A. From A measure down on side seam guideline the length of slacks desired. Dot.

B. Square a line from side seam guideline at each side of dot across paper. Label *ankle line*. Line should be parallel to crotch line.

C. Establish knee line halfway between hipline and ankle line. Label *knee line*.

D. Extend center front line parallel to side seam down to ankle line.

E. Square a line from D down to ankle line.

Note: The back of the slack leg is generally wider than the front. The amount will vary depending upon the shape and figure measurements and fit desired at crotch line.

F. To shape upper leg seam, lightly draw a straight line from knee line to crotch line on front and back of slacks.

G. At the center between knee line and crotch line, measure in ½" (1.27 cm). Dot.

H. Draw curved lines from knee line to crotch line at *back* and *front* touching dots (as illustrated).

I. To shape ankle, measure 1¼" (3.18 cm) on either side of *new side seam*. Dot each side.

J. Draw a straight line connecting dots to crotch line (heavier line).

K. Measure in 1¼" (3.18 cm) at ankle on back and front inner seams. Dot each side.

L. Draw a straight line connecting dots to knee line on each side.

Note: For a tighter fit at ankle, it is necessary to reduce width of the finished sloper at the *knee line* and *ankle line*. Amount of reduction varies depending upon fit, style, or effect desired.

M. Establish grainlines by squaring a line down from hipline on both front and back of slacks (as illustrated).

N. Establish crossmarks at side seam and inner leg seams at crotch and knee lines. See illustration.

O. Draft is now ready for testing in muslin.

P. Transfer corrections, if any, to draft.

SLACK SLOPER DEVELOPED FROM SKIRT SLOPER

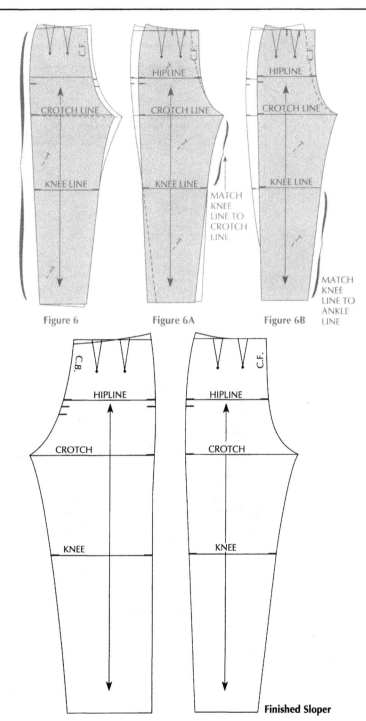

Figure 6

Figure 6A

MATCH
KNEE
LINE TO
CROTCH
LINE

Figure 6B

MATCH
KNEE
LINE TO
ANKLE
LINE

Finished Sloper

FIGURES 6, 6A, 6B

A. Copy draft onto oaktag. Cut on all finished lines. Notch waistline crossmarks. With awl indicate end of darts.

B. To notch hip, crotch and knee line crossmarks at side seam, pin front and back side seams together starting at hipline up to waistline and down to ankle. Both ends should match, if copied accurately. Adjust, if necessary, by compromising.

C. Notch crossmarks (Figure 6).

D. Separate slopers and notch center front and center back at hipline.

E. Match slopers on inner leg seam starting at knee line up to crotch line. If crotch line does not match, adjust by compromising (Figure 6A).

F. Notch knee line.

G. Match slopers on inner leg seams from knee line down to ankle line. If ankle lines do not match, adjust by compromising (Figure 6B).

SLACK SLOPER DEVELOPED FROM MEASUREMENTS

If a skirt sloper is not available, it is possible to develop the slacks sloper from measurements or from the fitted torso sloper. However, the use of the skirt sloper in developing slacks slopers is more accurate in fit, because the waistline curve and position of the side seams have been fitted to the figure.

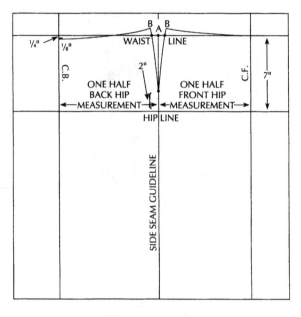

FIGURE 1

A. To prepare paper, refer to SLACKS SLOPER DEVELOPED FROM SKIRT SLOPER, Figure 1, A, B, and C.

B. Develop rectangle and label *all lines* and A at top of side seam guideline (as illustrated).

C. To determine side seam, on waistline from A measure in ½" (1.27 cm). Dot. Repeat on opposite side.

D. Place a dot 2" (5.08 cm) above hipline on side seam guideline.

E. To shape side seam, place a French curve to side seam and hipline touching 2" (5.08 cm) dot. Draw in curved hipline from this dot, ⅜" (0.95 cm) above waistline. Dot and label *B*. Repeat on opposite side.

F. Shape front waistline with hip curve ruler. Draw a slightly curved line from B to waistline.

Note: 1. Curved line must end approximately 3" (7.62 cm) from center front. *2.* Refer to SKIRT SLOPER WITH ONE DART, Figure 3, for placement of curved ruler.

G. Repeat for back waistline *with one exception:* lower waistline at center back ¼" (0.64 cm) and in ⅛" (0.32 cm) (short heavier line).

H. To complete slacks sloper, refer to SLACKS SLOPER DEVELOPED FROM SKIRT SLOPER starting with Figure 3.

SLACK SLOPER DEVELOPED FROM FITTED TORSO SLOPER

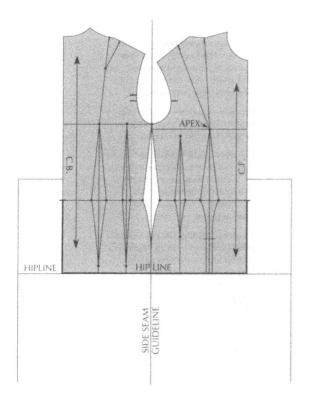

FIGURE 1

A. To prepare paper, refer to SLACKS SLOPER DEVELOPED FROM SKIRT SLOPER, Figure 1, A, B, and C.

B. Match hipline of front and back torso sloper to hipline on paper and side seams of slopers to side seam guideline.

C. Outline sloper from waistline down to hipline.

D. Remove sloper. To complete shaping of side seam and waistline refer to SLACKS SLOPER DEVELOPED FROM MEASUREMENT, Figure 1, C through G.

E. To complete slacks sloper, refer to SLACKS SLOPER DEVELOPED FROM SKIRT SLOPER starting with Figure 3.

SLACK SLOPER FOR
STRAIGHT HANGING SLACKS

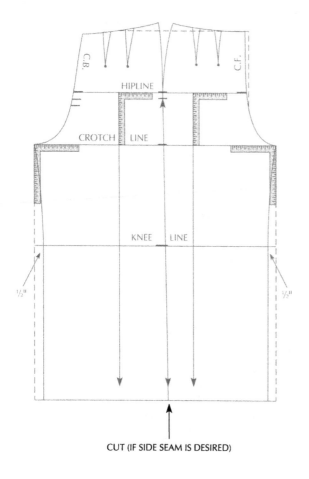

C.B.

C.F.

HIPLINE

CROTCH LINE

KNEE LINE

½"   ½"

CUT (IF SIDE SEAM IS DESIRED)

FIGURE 1

A. Copy upper section (crotch line to waistline) of slacks draft including darts and pleat plus side seam, new side seam, ankle line, knee line, and grainlines.

B. Square a line on draft from end of front and back crotchline to ankle line (broken lines).

C. For a slight shaping at the knee, if desired, measure in ½" (1.27 cm). Draw a curved line from crotch line to knee line, continuing line to ankle line parallel to broken line.

Note: 1. If cutting slacks without side seams and in stripe, plaid, or check fabric, waistline and center front may be cut on straight grain to avoid cutting into pattern of fabric (broken line). *2.* If a side seam is desired, cut apart on new side seam.

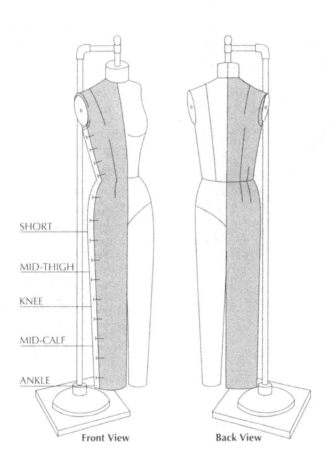

SHORT

MID-THIGH

KNEE

MID-CALF

ANKLE

Front View   Back View

JUMPSUIT SLOPER

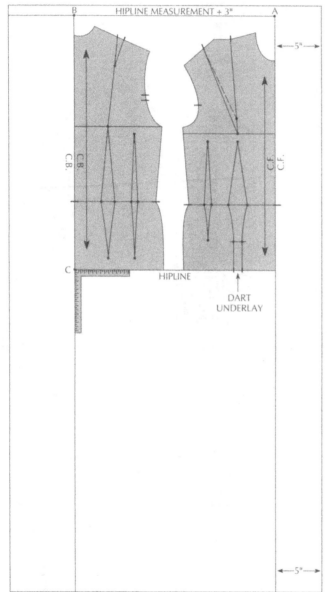

FIGURE 1

A. Cut paper approximately 35" × 64" (88.90 × 162.56 cm).

B. Draw two lines at a right angle 1" (2.54 cm) from top edge and 5" (12.70 cm) in from *right* edge of paper. Label vertical line *center front* and top of line *A*.

C. From *A* measure across front and back hip measurement of torso length slopers plus 3" (7.62 cm). Dot. Label *B*.

D. From *B* square a line parallel to center front the full length of paper. Label *center back*.

E. From *B* measure back length of torso sloper plus 3" (7.62 cm). Dot. Label *C*.

F. From *C* square a line across to center front. Label *hipline*.

G. Place front and back torso length slopers on paper as illustrated.

H. Outline slopers, crossmark back and front shoulder darts, armholes, waistline and dart underlay on front hipline. With awl indicate all darts except front and back side darts unless a very tight fitting garment is desired.

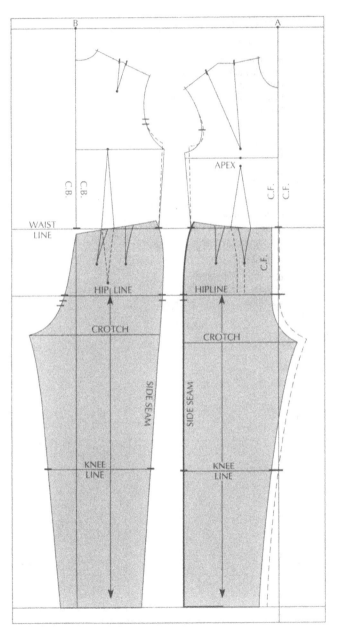

FIGURE 2

A. Remove slopers. Draw in all dartlines. Pencil in dots and connect waistline crossmarks and continue line to edges of paper. Label *waistline*.

Note: If a slack sloper is not available, the slack section can be developed directly on the draft. Refer to Slack Sloper Developed from Skirt Sloper, starting from Figure 5, page 116.

B. Match hipline and side seam of *back* slack sloper to hipline and side seam on draft.

C. Outline side seam, ankle, inner leg and crotch line, blending line from hipline into waistline at center back.

D. Indicate hipline and kneeline crossmarks at center back and side seam as illustrated.

Note: Do not indicate slack waistline or darts.

E. Remove back sloper. Connect kneeline crossmarks. Label *kneeline*.

F. Repeat same for front with one exception: The torso sloper hipline may be wider than the slack sloper due to the sloper size of the bustline which increases the dart underlay at the hipline. If this occurs:

> **1.** Outline side seam and one-half of ankle line (heavy line). Crossmark kneeline and hipline.
>
> **2.** Move sloper on hipline toward front until hipline touches center front line on draft.
>
> **3.** Outline remainder of ankle, inner leg and crotch lines and indicate crossmarks at hipline and kneeline. See broken line.
>
> **4.** Remove sloper. Connect kneeline crossmarks. Label *kneeline.*

JUMPSUIT SLOPER

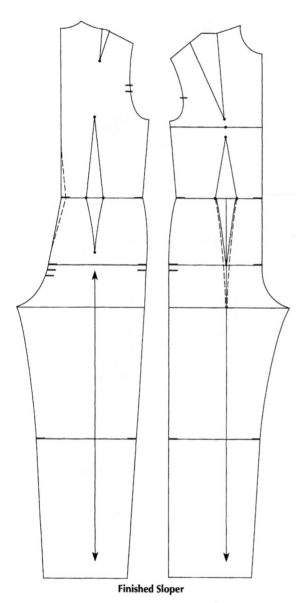

Finished Sloper

FIGURE 3

A. To complete true all lines.

B. If front waistline dart underlay at hipline is very deep, dart will need to be lengthened below hipline for a smooth fit. See broken lines.

C. Establish grainlines by squaring lines from hipline on front and back of slacks.

D. Draft is now ready to be tested in muslin.

E. Transfer corrections, if any, to draft and copy draft onto oaktag. Cut on all finished lines.

F. Notch all crossmarks and dartlines.

G. With awl indicate apex, end of darts and dartlines on waistline.

CONVERTING DRESS SLEEVE SLOPER TO BE USED ON SUIT OR COAT SLOPERS (⅛" SCALE)

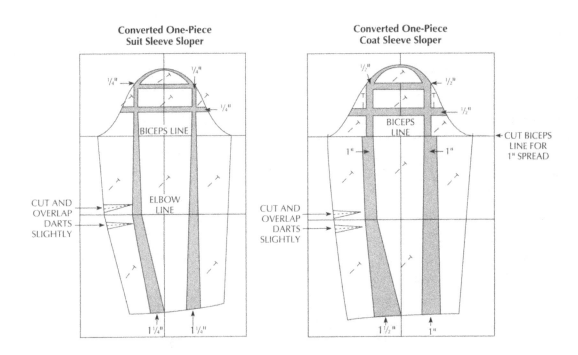

Converted One-Piece Suit Sleeve Sloper

Converted One-Piece Coat Sleeve Sloper

¼"   ¼"

½"   ½"

¼"   ¼"

½"   ½"

BICEPS LINE

BICEPS LINE

◄ CUT BICEPS LINE FOR 1" SPREAD

1"   1"

CUT AND OVERLAP DARTS SLIGHTLY

ELBOW LINE

CUT AND OVERLAP DARTS SLIGHTLY

1¼"   1¼"

1½"   1"

For a Two-Piece Suit or Coat Sleeve, Use Converted Suit or Coat Sleeve.

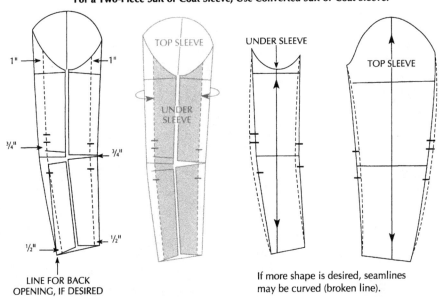

1"   1"

TOP SLEEVE

UNDER SLEEVE

TOP SLEEVE

¾"   ¾"

UNDER SLEEVE

½"   ½"

LINE FOR BACK OPENING, IF DESIRED

If more shape is desired, seamlines may be curved (broken line).

CONVERTING DRESS SLOPERS TO SUIT OR COAT SLOPERS (¼" SCALE)

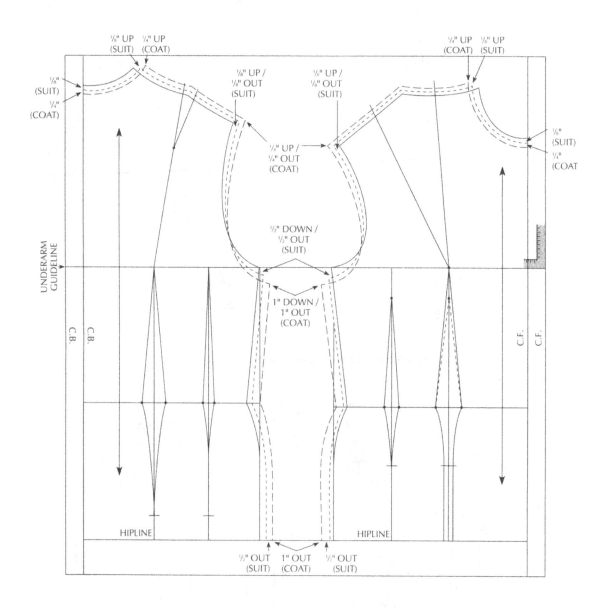

⅛" UP (SUIT) ¼" UP (COAT)

⅛" (SUIT) ¼" (COAT)

⅛" UP / ⅛" OUT (SUIT)

⅛" UP / ⅛" OUT (SUIT)

¼" UP (COAT) ⅛" UP (SUIT)

¼" UP / ¼" OUT (COAT)

⅛" (SUIT) ¼" (COAT

½" DOWN / ½" OUT (SUIT)

1" DOWN / 1" OUT (COAT)

UNDERARM GUIDELINE

C.B. C.B. C.B.

C.F. C.F.

HIPLINE   HIPLINE

½" OUT (SUIT)   1" OUT (COAT)   ½" OUT (SUIT)

CONVERTING DRESS SLOPERS TO SUIT OR COAT SLOPERS (¼" SCALE)

If a good dress sloper has been developed, it may be used as the foundation for a suit or coat sloper. The adjustments indicated in the illustrations, if carefully executed, will retain the original shape and fit of the garment.

The illustration indicates at a glance where ease or change is needed when converting dress slopers to suit or coat slopers. The measurements used in the illustration are average measurements for suits and coats. However, these measurements may be subject to change depending upon the weight of the fabric, the thickness of the lining, and the type of fit desired for a particular style or by an individual manufacturer.

FIGURE 1

A. Cut paper approximately 30" X 30" (76.20 X 76.20 cm).

B. Draw lines at left- and right-hand sides of paper 1" (2.54 cm) in from paper edge. Lines must be parallel to each other. Label *center front* and *center back* (as illustrated).

C. From top edge of paper, measure down 22" (55.88 cm) and square a line across paper. Label *underarm guideline*.

D. Place *torso sloper* on paper matching centers and underarm guideline. Outline (as illustrated).

E. To convert dress sloper into suit or coat sloper follow measurements illustrated on draft. All measurements are measured down, up or out from dress sloper lines (solid lines).

METRIC CONVERSION TABLE
(Inches to Centimeters)

Inches		1/16	1/8	1/4	3/8	1/2	5/8	3/4	7/8
		0.16	0.32	0.64	0.95	1.27	1.59	1.91	2.22
1	2.54	2.70	2.86	3.18	3.49	3.81	4.13	4.45	4.76
2	5.08	5.24	5.40	5.72	6.03	6.35	6.67	6.99	7.30
3	7.62	7.78	7.94	8.26	8.57	8.89	9.21	9.53	9.84
4	10.16	10.32	10.48	10.80	11.11	11.43	11.75	12.07	12.38
5	12.70	12.86	13.02	13.34	13.65	13.97	14.29	14.61	14.92
6	15.24	15.40	15.56	15.88	16.19	16.51	16.83	17.15	17.46
7	17.78	17.94	18.10	18.42	18.73	19.05	19.37	19.69	20.00
8	20.32	20.48	20.64	20.96	21.27	21.59	21.91	22.23	22.54
9	22.86	23.02	23.18	23.50	23.81	24.13	24.45	24.77	25.08
10	25.40	25.56	25.72	26.04	26.35	26.67	26.99	27.31	27.62
11	27.94	28.10	28.26	28.58	28.89	29.21	29.53	29.85	30.16
12	30.48	30.64	30.80	31.12	31.43	31.75	32.02	32.39	32.70
13	33.02	33.18	33.34	33.66	33.97	34.29	34.61	34.93	35.24
14	35.56	35.72	35.88	36.20	36.51	36.83	37.15	37.47	37.78
15	38.10	38.26	38.42	38.74	39.05	39.37	36.69	40.01	40.32
16	40.64	40.80	40.96	41.28	41.59	41.91	42.23	42.55	42.86
17	43.18	43.34	43.50	43.82	44.13	44.45	44.77	45.09	45.40
18	45.72	45.88	46.04	46.36	46.67	46.99	47.31	47.63	47.94
19	48.26	48.42	48.58	48.90	49.21	49.53	49.85	50.17	50.48
20	50.80	50.96	51.12	51.44	51.75	52.07	52.39	52.71	53.02
21	53.34	53.50	53.66	53.98	54.29	54.61	54.93	55.25	55.56
22	55.88	56.04	56.20	56.52	56.83	57.15	57.47	57.79	58.10
23	58.42	58.58	58.74	59.06	59.37	59.69	60.01	60.33	60.64
24	60.96	61.12	61.28	61.60	61.91	62.23	62.55	62.87	63.18
25	63.50	63.66	63.82	64.14	64.45	64.77	65.09	65.41	65.72
26	66.04	66.20	66.36	66.68	66.99	67.31	67.63	67.95	68.26
27	68.58	68.74	68.90	69.22	69.53	69.85	70.17	70.49	70.80
28	71.12	71.28	71.44	71.76	72.07	72.39	72.71	73.03	73.34
29	73.66	73.82	73.98	74.30	74.61	74.93	75.25	75.57	75.88
30	76.20	76.36	76.52	76.84	77.15	77.47	77.79	78.11	78.42
31	78.74	78.90	79.06	79.38	79.69	80.01	80.33	80.65	80.96
32	81.28	81.44	81.60	81.92	82.23	82.55	82.87	83.19	83.50
33	83.82	83.98	84.14	84.46	84.77	85.09	85.41	85.73	86.04
34	86.36	86.52	86.68	87.00	87.31	87.63	87.95	88.27	88.58
35	88.90	89.06	89.22	89.54	89.85	90.17	90.49	90.81	91.12
36	91.44	91.60	91.76	92.08	92.39	92.71	93.03	93.35	93.66
37	93.98	94.14	94.30	94.62	94.93	95.25	95.57	95.89	96.20
38	96.52	96.68	96.84	97.16	97.47	97.79	98.11	98.43	98.74
39	99.06	99.22	99.38	99.70	100.01	100.33	100.65	100.97	101.28
40	101.60	101.76	101.92	102.24	102.55	102.87	103.19	103.51	103.83
41	104.14	104.30	104.46	104.78	105.09	105.41	105.73	106.05	106.36
42	106.68	106.84	107.00	107.32	107.63	107.95	108.27	108.59	108.90
43	109.22	109.38	109.54	109.86	110.17	110.49	110.81	111.13	111.44
44	111.76	111.92	112.08	112.40	112.71	113.03	113.35	113.67	113.98
45	114.30	114.46	114.62	114.94	115.25	115.57	115.89	116.21	116.52
46	116.84	117.00	117.16	117.48	117.79	118.11	118.43	118.75	119.06
47	119.38	119.54	119.70	120.02	120.33	120.65	120.97	121.29	121.60
48	121.92	122.08	122.24	122.56	122.87	123.19	123.51	123.83	124.14
49	124.46	124.62	124.78	125.10	125.41	125.73	126.05	126.37	126.68
50	127.00	127.16	127.32	127.64	127.95	128.27	128.59	128.91	129.22
51	129.54	129.70	129.86	130.18	130.49	130.81	131.13	131.45	131.76
52	132.08	132.24	132.40	132.72	133.03	133.35	133.67	133.99	134.30
53	134.62	134.78	134.94	135.26	135.57	135.89	136.21	136.53	136.84
54	137.16	137.32	137.48	137.80	138.11	138.43	138.75	139.07	139.38
55	139.70	139.86	140.02	140.34	140.65	140.97	141.29	141.61	141.92
56	142.24	142.40	142.56	142.88	143.19	143.51	143.83	144.15	144.46
57	144.78	144.94	145.10	145.42	145.73	146.05	146.37	146.69	147.00
58	147.32	147.48	147.64	147.96	148.27	148.59	148.91	149.23	149.54
59	149.86	150.02	150.18	150.50	150.81	151.13	151.45	151.77	152.08
60	152.40	152.56	152.72	153.04	153.35	153.67	153.99	154.31	154.62

CPSIA information can be obtained
at www.ICGtesting.com
Printed in the USA
LVHW021225190123
737423LV00006B/495